Michael Kutschke

Ensemble Learning for Method-Call Recommendation

AF138179

Michael Kutschke

Ensemble Learning for Method-Call Recommendation

Exploring features for a smart code completion

Reihe Formalwissenschaften

Impressum / Imprint

Bibliografische Information der Deutschen Nationalbibliothek: Die Deutsche Nationalbibliothek verzeichnet diese Publikation in der Deutschen Nationalbibliografie; detaillierte bibliografische Daten sind im Internet über http://dnb.d-nb.de abrufbar.

Alle in diesem Buch genannten Marken und Produktnamen unterliegen warenzeichen-, marken- oder patentrechtlichem Schutz bzw. sind Warenzeichen oder eingetragene Warenzeichen der jeweiligen Inhaber. Die Wiedergabe von Marken, Produktnamen, Gebrauchsnamen, Handelsnamen, Warenbezeichnungen u.s.w. in diesem Werk berechtigt auch ohne besondere Kennzeichnung nicht zu der Annahme, dass solche Namen im Sinne der Warenzeichen- und Markenschutzgesetzgebung als frei zu betrachten wären und daher von jedermann benutzt werden dürften.

Bibliographic information published by the Deutsche Nationalbibliothek: The Deutsche Nationalbibliothek lists this publication in the Deutsche Nationalbibliografie; detailed bibliographic data are available in the Internet at http://dnb.d-nb.de.

Any brand names and product names mentioned in this book are subject to trademark, brand or patent protection and are trademarks or registered trademarks of their respective holders. The use of brand names, product names, common names, trade names, product descriptions etc. even without a particular marking in this works is in no way to be construed to mean that such names may be regarded as unrestricted in respect of trademark and brand protection legislation and could thus be used by anyone.

Coverbild / Cover image: www.ingimage.com

Verlag / Publisher:
AV Akademikerverlag
ist ein Imprint der / is a trademark of
OmniScriptum GmbH & Co. KG
Heinrich-Böcking-Str. 6-8, 66121 Saarbrücken, Deutschland / Germany
Email: info@akademikerverlag.de

Herstellung: siehe letzte Seite /
Printed at: see last page
ISBN: 978-3-639-62699-5

Table of Contents

Chapter 1

Introduction

Today's software development is highly influenced and accelerated through the usage of tools. Integrated Development Environments (IDEs) are programs which incorporate vast amounts of different tools, trying to allow a developer to be maximally efficient. Eclipse[1], an open source IDE, includes tools ranging from syntax highlighting to version control systems. One of these tool systems is code completion - an assistant for developers to increase typing speed, explore new APIs, handle errors and just make life easier. Current research tries to improve on existing tools by exploiting implicit information and make it available to developers. This thesis goes in the same direction, and explores various context information that can be used to make code completion assistants better. We want to answer the question what context information is best suited for code completion, whether this is type-dependent, and how they can be combined in a joint model.

We will first introduce the subject and discuss the state of the art. We will then introduce terminology we use later in the thesis. We present the context information that we use to predict a developer's intent. We then evaluate the models we get using this context information. Afterwards, we focus on combining those models to further improve the proposals of the code completion.

---

[1]http://www.eclipse.org

1

1.1 Code Completion

Word processors have word completion [GVA06], search engines have query auto-completion [Sho13]. E-mail programs complete e-mail addresses for an easier access of the address book. All of these have in common that they have the goal of saving keystrokes and minimizing errors to increase the productivity of the user and the usability of the program.

Code-completion assistants are one of the tools found in most modern IDEs. Similar to completion features of browsers, word processors and other applications, they aim at accelerating the development by reducing the necessary keystrokes. Contrary to word completion for unstructured text, the structured nature of source code allows for much more accurate proposals than is possible for unstructured text. Additionally, code-completion assistants are commonly used by developers to gain knowledge about unknown APIs (application programmer interface) by browsing the proposed items. Thus code completion fulfills more purposes than just saving keystrokes or avoiding typing errors. Improving the code completion also means improving the rate at which a new API can be learned and mastered by a developer. Murphy et al. [MKF06] found that the code completion is used as much as basic editing commands like copy and paste. Still, most IDEs sort completion proposals alphabetically [HWM09] and don't take into account context information (see Figure 1.1).

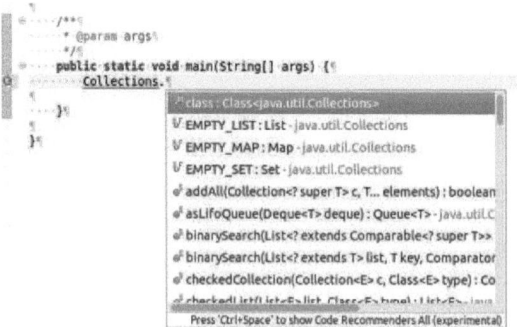

Figure 1.1: Code completion in the Eclipse IDE. Proposals are sorted alphabetically.

1.2 Motivation

In this thesis, we will focus on method-call recommendation. There has been, to our knowledge, only little research in this area, although code completion is such a frequently used tool. Some research has been done on how using context information can improve code completion [Bru12][Ama13][HH11]. Building on these works, we propose several types of previously unused context information that we expect to be discriminative for method usage. Also, we explore how good models based on just one of these context features can already predict the correct methods.

Models that exploit a lot of different context information suffer from several problems: First of all, more context means exponentially less examples that share a given context. This is also commonly called the "curse of dimensionality" [Bis06]. Second, complex models consume much more memory than simple models, especially when different parts of the context are not modeled to be independent. This comes from more free parameters of the model that need to be stored. Many free parameters also render a model prone to overfitting; overfitting occurs when a model is too adapted to the training data, and ultimately fails on the test data because it does not manage to generalize to the unseen.

To see how good our proposed simple models work in combination, we explore a simple type-dependent linear-combination scheme. This implicitly assumes conditional independence between the different parts of the context, given the method. While this certainly does not hold, this assumption reduces the amount of free parameters to a minimum. We compare different approaches to learn an optimal linear combination to a simple averaging scheme.

1.3 State of the Art

In this section, we present prior research related to our work. We present those works that we are aware of, and that fall in the area of intelligent code completion.

3

Eclipse Code Recommenders [Bru12]   Eclipse Code Recommenders[2] is a set of
IDE plugins including a method-call completion. The ranking is done through type-
dependent probabilistic models mined from example bytecode. The Code-Recommenders
models are based on patterns found in the source code, methods that appear together
often. In his PhD thesis, Marcel Bruch [Bru12] evaluates a modified version of a
k-Nearest-Neighbors algorithm for learning these patterns. Of the features described
in Section 2, they use two in their thesis: *calls*, and *override context*. In the current
version of the Code Recommenders tool, the *definition kind* is also used. The dataset
used in his evaluation comprises clients of the SWT framework inside the Eclipse
3.4.2 repository. Since Eclipse 3.8, Eclipse Code Recommenders is distributed together with the Eclipse IDE for Java Developers.

Code Completion Based on Implicit User Feedback [Ama13]   Sven Amann [Ama13]
presents a system for method-call recommendation based on implicit user feedback.
Instead of learning from existing code, he proposed to learn from the actual completions that developers choose. His thesis uses a modified version of the kNN-algorithm
as well. The thesis uses a variety of features, *override context* being the one in common with our thesis. Sven Amann's thesis shows that there are a range of features
in source code that are very discriminative, but are hard to retrieve after compila-
tion. Specifically, the structure of the AST is exploited, which is not, for the most
part, reflected in bytecode. This includes the expected return type and control flow
structures.

Improving Code Completion with Program History [RL08]   Robbes et al. [RL08]
use the program history as a source of data to improve their code completion. They
use a system that captures a developer's programming history on a syntactic level,
such as creation of classes, insertion of new methods, etc. (as opposed to text-based
change that is used in version control systems [SL]). They show that proposing re-
cently used methods or classes greatly increases the accuracy of code-completion
assistants, even if type information is ignored. Their approach is however targeted
at the single developer and offers no assistance for learning new APIs as opposed to

---

[2]http://www.eclipse.org/recommenders

approaches that learn models from existing source code.

Recommending API Methods Based on Identifier Contexts [HH11]   Heinemann
et al. [HH11] mine the source code for identifiers that appear in a certain amount of
source code lines preceding the site where the object usage appears. They then use
an algorithm based on nearest neighbors to recommend method calls that appeared in
similar contexts. This is again similar to our approach in that information is extracted
from the method context. Heinemann et al. mine from source code, while we mine
the bytecode. While mining the source code provides context information that is
not anymore present in bytecode, mining from bytecode has the advantage of being
applicable to code that is not available in source form, as well as being able to mine
from clients that are not Java-based (e.g. Scala).

It is interesting to note the differences between the works discussed above: One
learns from the byte code [Bru12], one learns from relevance feedback [Ama13], one
learns from the change history [RL08], and one learns from the source code [HH11].
We see there is a huge design space, that leads to quite different solutions. In our
thesis, we use the bytecode as source of our data, and thus follow in the steps of
Marcel Bruch's thesis [Bru12].

1.4   Bayesian Networks

Probabilistic models are the models of choice for many problems. They are readily
learned from data and easy to grasp and argue about. Because of this, probabilistic
models have been used by Marcel Bruch [Bru12] in his tool Code Recommenders as
well as by Heinemann et al. [HH11] in the form of *Hidden Markov Models*. The com-
putation of the probability of an event given an observation about the world is simple,
and relies on the following two equations, the *sum rule* and the *product rule* [Bis06]:

$$p(a) = \sum_b p(a, b) \qquad \text{(sum rule)}$$

$$p(a, b) = p(b|a)p(a) \qquad \text{(product rule)}$$

These two equations are enough to solve any inference tasks that come up.

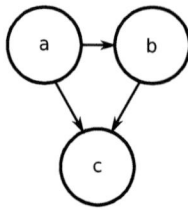
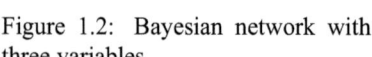

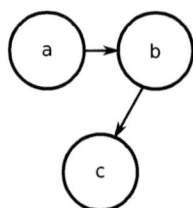

Figure 1.2: Bayesian network with three variables

Figure 1.3: c is independent of a given b

A way to visualize and represent a probability distribution over multiple variables is a *Bayesian network*. A Bayesian network is a directed acyclic graph whose vertices correspond to the random variables of the distribution and the edges capture the relationship between those variables. It visualizes how the distribution can be decomposed into factors, using the product rule [Bis06].

For example, given some distribution $p(a, b, c)$, we see that after applying the product rule, we get Equation 1.1.

$$p(a, b, c) = p(c|a, b)p(a, b) \tag{1.1}$$

Applying the rule a second time yields Equation 1.2.

$$p(a, b, c) = p(c|a, b)p(b|a)p(a) \tag{1.2}$$

Expressing this as Bayesian network as seen in Figure 1.2, we get three vertices a, b, c, with edges arranged in a way that those vertices are connected that depend on each other according to the factorization. c depends on a and b, and b in turn depends on a.

If we now assume that, for our particular example distribution, c is independent of a given b (which is mathematically expressed by Equation 1.3), we can simplify the Bayesian network to the form shown in Figure 1.3, which corresponds to the factorization shown in Equation 1.4.

$$p(c|a, b) = p(c|b) \tag{1.3}$$

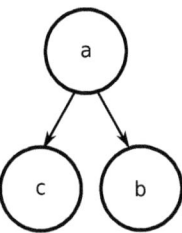

Figure 1.4: Generic Bayesian network with naive Bayes assumption

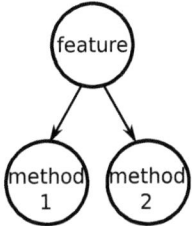

Figure 1.5: Network with naive Bayes assumption applied to the different methods

$$p(a, b, c) = p(c|b)p(b|a)p(a) \tag{1.4}$$

Representing a probability distribution as Bayesian network has several advantages. First, by allowing usage of the conditional-independence relations between variables, it is a very efficient representation, as this reduces the parameters of the model that need to be stored. Then, being a graphical model, it is easy to discuss and argue about. Third, it easily allows assumptions of conditional independence to be made during the modeling process. These assumptions are wrong most of the time, but greatly reduce the parameters that need to be learned and thus avoid *overfitting*. Overfitting is the behavior of a model with many parameters to predict the training data well, but then fail on other data as it is too specialized on the training data.

1.5 Naive-Bayes Assumption

In this thesis, we use the naive-Bayes assumption for all our models. Bayesian networks subject to this assumption have a simple structure as shown in Figure 1.4. There is one "root" vertex and several "leaf" vertices. This means the "leaf" variables are assumed to be independent of each other given the "root" variable; this is called the *naive-Bayes assumption*.

Typically in machine learning, the root variable is the class to be predicted, while the leaf variables are the possible observations: the features. We also use the naive-Bayes assumption in our models; but our two different schemes for the Bayesian net-

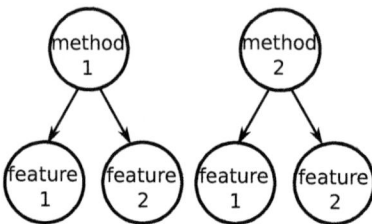

Figure 1.6: Bayesian network for set-valued features, subject to naive-Bayes assumption

works of our base models as described in Section 2 differ from this common method. For features that can only have one observed state at a time, e.g. the method that is overridden, we use the scheme depicted in Figure 1.5. The feature variable is used as root and the methods to be predicted as leaves. Note that we are not trying to predict the one method that the developer needs at this point, but rather the set of methods he will need. We compare the methods by their probability of them being used in the given context. Since multiple methods can be rightly used in a context, and the developer might actually need all of them, it does not make sense to model the proposed method as being exclusive. Rather, it is modeled as being potentially set-valued. This is consistent to prior work, especially Code Recommenders[3]. For the features that are set-valued, for example the parts of the method name, we use one instance of a naive-Bayesian network per method to be predicted, with that method as root; the possible feature values are the boolean-valued leaves. An example of this is shown in figure 1.6.

Although the naive-Bayes assumption is in the most cases wrong, this assumption is still frequently used, as it makes models significantly smaller and easier to train. Zhang shows that naive-Bayes classifier work well in many cases even though the naive-Bayes assumption is wrong [Zha04]. The naive-Bayes assumption thus is a good candidate for implementation of simple models.

---

[3]http://www.eclipse.org/recommenders

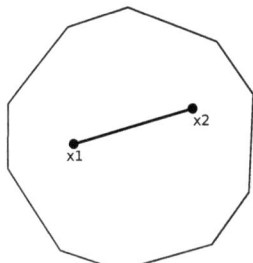

Figure 1.7: Convex set illustration

1.6 Optimization

In Section 4, we present different approaches to learn ensemble rankers based on mathematical optimization. In this section we describe a few optimization basics.

Constrained optimization is the optimization of a function $f(x) : \mathbb{R}^n \to \mathbb{R}$, called *objective function*, subject to certain constraints, denoted in Problem 1.5 as $x \in X$. Points that satisfy those constraints are called *feasible*. The set of feasible points X is called the *feasible set*.

$$\begin{aligned} \underset{x \in \mathbb{R}^n}{\text{minimize}} \quad & f(x) \\ \text{subject to} \quad & \\ & x \in X \end{aligned} \qquad (1.5)$$

The existence of an optimum is guaranteed if the objective function is continuous and the feasible set is compact [Lan04]. Compactness means the set is bounded and closed.

1.6.1 Convexity

Convexity is an important concept for optimization to guarantee that local optima that are found are also global optima [Lan04]. A set is called convex if and only if

$$x_1, x_2 \in X \implies \forall \alpha \in [0, 1] : \alpha x_1 + (1 - \alpha)x_2 \in X. \qquad (1.6)$$

9

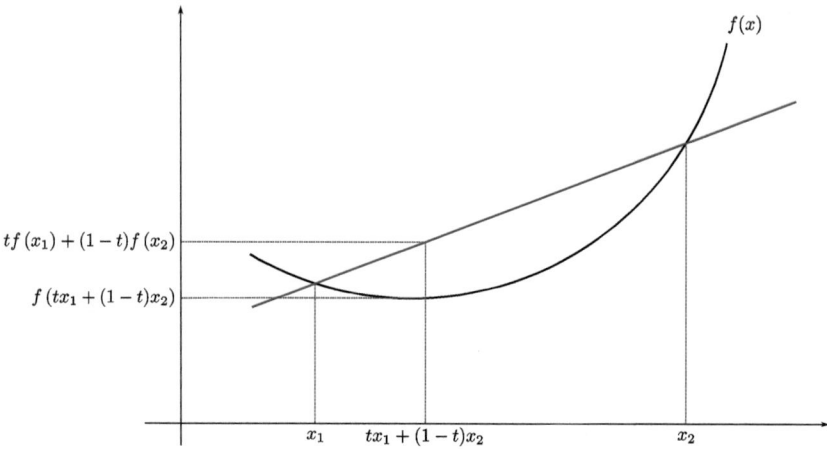

Figure 1.8: Convex function illustration, Eli Osherovich, June 30, 2010 `http://commons.wikimedia.org/wiki/File:ConvexFunction.svg`, CC-BY-SA 3.0

This means, in other words, that every point between two points of the set is also in the set (see Figure 1.7).

Figure 1.8 shows a *convex function*. Convexity for a function $f(x)$ means that the set $\{(x, y)|y \geq f(x)\}$ is convex, or in other terms

$$f(\alpha x_1 + (1 - \alpha)x_2) \leq \alpha f(x_1) + (1 - \alpha)f(x_2), \forall \alpha \in [0, 1]. \qquad (1.7)$$

As we stated above, local optima of convex functions are also globally optimal [Lan04]. Local optima of convex functions over non-convex sets of points are not necessarily globally optimal; however, local optima of convex objective functions over convex sets are also globally optimal [Lan04].

1.6.2 Linear Optimization

A special form of optimization problem is the linear optimization problem, also called *linear program*. An optimization problem is called *linear*, if and only if both the objective function and the constraints are linear:

$$\underset{x\in\mathbb{R}^n}{\text{minimize}} \quad c^T x$$

$$\text{subject to} \qquad\qquad (1.8)$$

$$Ax \leq b$$

Every linear constraint implies a hyperplane that separates feasible from infeasible points. The intersection of these half-spaces is a convex polytope like the one shown in Figure 1.7. The feasible set being convex, a local optimum of a linear program is also global.

One other important property that make linear optimization easier than its non-linear counterpart is that if there is a minimum, then one of the corners of the feasible set (which is a polytope) is minimal [BT97].

The simplex algorithm is an algorithm for solving linear optimization problems [BT97]. It searches the optimum by examining the corners of the feasible set in an order that guarantees non-decreasing objective-function value.

1.6.3   Non-linear Optimization

A general non-linear optimization problem is a problem with continuous objective function and continuous constraints.

$$\underset{x\in\mathbb{R}}{\text{minimize}} \quad f(x)$$

$$\text{subject to} \qquad\qquad (1.9)$$

$$g(x) \leq 0$$
$$h(x) = 0$$

This problem is, in general, not convex; there is no guarantee that an algorithm will find the global minimum [BSS06]. There are different algorithms to find local optima; we use a quadratic penalty method to turn the constrained Problem 1.9 into the unconstrained Problem 1.10.

$$\underset{x \in \mathbb{R}}{\text{minimize}} \quad f(x) + \alpha \pi(x)$$
$$\pi(x) = ||h(x)||_2^2 + ||max(0, g(x))||_2^2. \tag{1.10}$$

There is, to our knowledge, no existing implementation of a constrained non-linear optimization problem solver which fit our needs of being written in Java and being Open Source. We therefore chose this method for our exploratory work as it is easy to implement. An implementation of an unconstrained problem solver is available in the Apache Commons Math library[4].

The quadratic penalty method solves the constrained problem by solving the unconstrained problem multiple times, each time increasing the penalty parameter α and using the latest optimum as new starting point. It has been shown that with α increasing, the solution converges to a feasible point which is locally optimal [BSS06].

---

[4]http://commons.apache.org/proper/commons-math/

Chapter 2

Features

Listing 2.1 shows an example code of a Button that shows how many Listeners are registered. There is a List *listeners* that maintains the information about the registered listeners. The class overrides the methods *addListener* and *removeListener*, and adds or removes the listeners to that list. It then updates the Button's label to reflect that change. From this example, we already can learn something about *List*s. We could deduce that the methods *add* and *remove* as well as *size* are used more often than methods like *retainAll* or *wait*. Recommending methods that are used more often than others is a simple way to improve the code completion.

On the other hand, we learn that adding an element to a collection is as likely as removing it. Our intuition tells us, however, that the method *addListener* should add an object to the list, while *removeListener* should remove it. There is context information that influences how likely a method is going to be called. This includes the method name, the class hierarchy, other called methods, the way an object was created, etc.

In the following, we present different features, some of which have been examined in prior work, while others have not. We use each of these features to construct a probabilistic model of the correlations between these features and used method calls. We will later use these models to rank the methods according to their probability in the given context. During this thesis, we will refer to these models as *base models* as opposed to the combined models we discuss later.

The base models are:

frequency the relative frequency of a method

calls uses the methods already called inside the method body

override context uses the method that is overridden by the enclosing method

definition kind uses whether the object was returned by a method or passed in as parameter

defining method uses the method or constructor from which the object was returned

method name uses the parts of the method name, split by camel case

package name uses the last part of the package name

parameter types uses the available parameter types of the enclosing method

2.1 Frequency

To assert the value of our features, we need a *baseline* model to compare them with during the evaluation. A baseline is a minimally complex model serving as comparison for the other models. We use a model based on the frequency of the used methods as baseline.

As stated above, we can get the idea from Listing 2.1 that *List.size()* is a method that is commonly used. However, in an alphabetic order, it is one of the last methods that appear, even after rarely used methods like *notify()* and *hashCode()*. Even when narrowed down to methods whose names start with *s*, the rare method *set* is still listed at the top. Marcel Bruch [Bru12] and Sven Amann [Ama13] have shown that a completion system ranking methods according to frequency generally outperforms the alphabetic order.

A model based on frequency will list those methods at the top that are used most often. However, it completely ignores available context information. For example, in Listing 2.1, lines 27-32, it is clear to a human reader that the code completion should propose a *remove* method rather than an *add* method because we are in the scope of a method whose name is *removeListener*. A frequency based model, ignorant of this

14

override context	definition kind
method name	defining method
package name	calls
parameter types	

```java
1  package examples.swt. widgets ;
2
3  import java.util.ArrayList;
4  import java.util.List;
5
6  import org.eclipse.swt.widgets.Button;
7  import org.eclipse.swt.widgets.Composite;
8  import org.eclipse.swt.widgets.Listener;
9
10 public class SWTExampleButton extends Button {
11
12     List<Listener> listeners = new ArrayList<Listener>() ;
13
14     public SWTExampleButton(Composite parent, int style) {
15         super(parent, style);
16     }
17
18     @ Override
19     public void addListener ( int eventType, Listener listener) {
20         super.addListener(eventType, listener);
21         listeners. add (listener);
22         int size = listeners. size ();
23         this.setText("Listeners:␣" + size);
24     }
25
26     @ Override
27     public void removeListener ( int eventType, Listener listener) {
28         super.removeListener(eventType, listener);
29         listeners. remove (listener);
30         int size = listeners. size ();
31         this.setText("Listeners:␣" + size);
32     }
33 }
```

Listing 2.1: Example program

context, would still propose *add* over *remove* if the model says developers more often add things to a list than removing something.

Throughout this thesis, we will refer to this model as *baseline* or *frequency baseline*. Where we see fit, we abbreviate this to *freq*, for example in plots.

2.2   Calls

On lines 21-23 of Listing 2.1, there is a modification of a collection through the *add* method, after which a variable depending on the size of the collection is updated. This indicates that there is a potential correlation between calls that modify state, like *List.add* and *List.remove*, and methods that query the state, like *List.size()*. On the other hand, we expect it is rather rare to call *List.add* and *List.remove* in the same method.

Marcel Bruch [Bru12] showed that there are patterns how developers use different types, making the usage of different methods correlated. Those correlations were successfully exploited by clustering methods that frequently appear together, and then transforming this clustering into a probabilistic model. We don't cluster methods in this thesis, and hope to lose less information because of that.

We will refer to this model as *calls*. We expect that this feature will perform well for types that typically get used multiple times within a method. One example of this is user-interface widgets. Typically such an object needs to go through an extensive initialization procedure to connect it to other parts of the user interface. A button's size is adjusted, it is initialized with a label, there are listeners that want to be informed when the user clicks the button. On the other hand, when no call has yet been made, this feature cannot exploit any context, degrading it to the frequency baseline. There are types which are typically only used once within a method. For example, *java.lang.Class* is used just once 1209 out of 1383 times in our evaluation data. In such cases, the model again degenerates to the frequency baseline. We expect that models using different context information to work better in those cases.

16

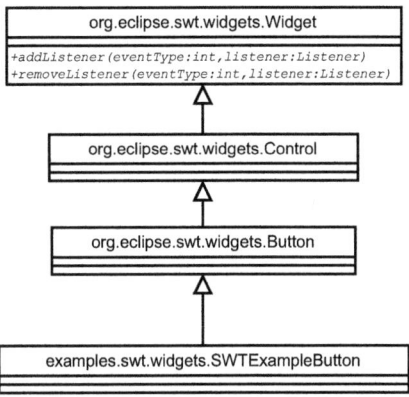

Figure 2.1: Class hierarchy of the example class from Listing 2.1

2.3 Override Context

We call the "topmost" definition of the surrounding method the *override context*; if the method does not override anything, we use the constant *UNKNOWN_METHOD*. The override context represents a part of the intention of the method. Although overriding often adds or changes functionality of the overridden method, the basic intention of the method remains the same and untouched. From the intent, we can deduce what methods are likely to be called.

Figure 2.1 shows the class hierarchy of the *SWTExampleButton* class from Listing 2.1. We see that the original definition of the *addListener* and *removeListener* is three steps up in the hierarchy. In Listing 2.1, when triggering code completion at line 22, the override context would thus be *Widget.addListener(int,Listener)*, as Widget is the first class in the hierarchy that defines *addListener(int,Listener)*. In this context, it is arguably more likely to call *List.add* and even less likely to call *List.remove*.

We expect this feature to be helpful in the context of frameworks, like SWT, and less in the context of libraries, e.g. Apache Commons. However, this feature represents, in a certain sense, the bridge between the two. It may well be that a type not included in the framework (e.g. java.util.List) is used differently in different override contexts (e.g. it is maybe more likely that a collection is changed in a method that gets notified of user input). Using the topmost definition is a design choice. On the one hand, there are less top-level definitions than there are overridden definitions in total. On the other hand, we found that the top-most context helps better at predicting method calls than the "lowest" definition, probably due to better generalization.

This feature suffers from the problem that with increasing amounts of available code, the state space will explode. This leads to infeasible model sizes as well as overfitting.

For the purpose of brevity, we will refer to this model as *context* or *override context*.

2.4 Definition Kind

An object can be obtained in multiple ways. In lines 19-24 of Listing 2.1, there is a List object that is a field of the surrounding class, and a Listener that got passed in as parameter to the method. We argue that the way an object is obtained influences its usage. A List field is more likely to be mutated than a List parameter, which is often just a container for a multi-valued parameter, and not mutated.

For every type of creation we introduce a symbolic value:

NEW the object has been created by a constructor call

PARAMETER the object has been passed to the method as parameter

METHOD_RETURN the object has been returned by a call to another method

FIELD the object is a field of the surrounding class

THIS the object is the one the surrounding method has been invoked on

UNKNOWN for the cases where the static analysis cannot determine where the object comes from

This feature is supposedly particularly resistant against overfitting because of the highly limited state space. On the other hand, we expect that it is strongly type-dependent which one of the possible values appear. A *java.util.List* will seldom be

18

found with a NEW definition kind, because *List* is an interface. In our data, we found 13 NEW kinds out of 6071 *List* usages, and 0 THIS kinds. On the other hand, the concrete type *java.util.ArrayList* should most of the time be instantiated inside the method. And indeed, 2993 out of 3635 *ArrayList* usages belong to the NEW kind, but only 31 are PARAMETER. We expect that the more contexts a type is used in with regard to definition kind, the more useful a definition-kind model will be.

We will refer to this model as *definition kind*, and abbreviate it to *kind* where we see fit.

2.5 Defining Method

We define the *defining method* as the method (or constructor) from which the object was returned/constructed; for a parameter object, this is the surrounding method. If the defining method cannot be determined (for example for a field), this feature has a null value. As an example, for the List object *listeners* in Listing 2.1, if it was defined inside one of the methods instead of a being a field, the defining method would be the constructor *java.util.ArrayList()*.

Initializing a collection with a fixed size or with the values of another collection may be a sign that this collection is not going to change. This may make calls to *add* less likely, and increase the likelihood of *get, iterator* and potentially *retainAll*, among others. We thus expect this feature to work well on types with multiple constructors, as well as types that get returned by diverse sources. Interfaces tend to be returned more often than their implemented counterparts; we thus expect the state space of the defining-method feature to be larger for interfaces than for their implementations. This would allow for a finer distinction, but bear the risk of overfitting.

Defining method and definition kind share some information. Through the defining method, it can be determined whether an object was created through a constructor or returned by some method. Although the defining-method feature has no sensible value for a field, most objects that are not fields will have a defining method. A null value indicates a field. Thus, defining method can be seen as a specialized version of definition kind, except for objects that are parameters, which cannot be recognized without having the knowledge what the surrounding method is.

19

We will refer to this model as *defining method* or short *def*.

2.6 Method Name

The method name encodes (or should encode) parts of the developer's intention as to the method's functionality. While methods often have (or should have) long, more or less unique names, there are parts of the name that reappear frequently among similar methods. An example of this are the omnipresent setter and getter methods, which start by "set" and "get" by convention. We assume, for example, that collections are more likely to be modified in methods that contain "set" or "add" in their name, while getter methods are more likely to be called in methods that contain "get".

There is structure in method names, apart from just being an identifier. We use the parts of the method name as features; we discern the different parts by assuming the names follow the CamelCase notation. For example, the method name parts of the method *addListener* on line 19 of Listing 2.1 are "add" and "listener".

This feature is similar to override context. The same override context, if there is one, implies the same method name. On the other hand, the same method name does not imply the same override context. Thus method name, within limits, can be seen as a more general version of override context. We expect that this should translate to a better performance of models based on the method name.

We will refer to this model as *names* where we see fit.

2.7 Package Name

Packages serve the organization of source code; they convey a very high-level idea of the structure and intention of the code. Similar intentions may call for similar methods.

It does not make sense to use the fully qualified package name as feature, as it should be unique for every project. Instead, we use the last part of the package name, which should contain the most precise information. For the example class in Listing 2.1 this would be *"widgets"*. We argue that classes that are in a package ending with this name should represent similar things, even though they might not subclass the

20

same classes, nor even classes from the same framework. Still, we expect this feature to be less useful than the others as it represents the broadest context of all the features.

For brevity, we refer to this model as *package*.

2.8 Parameter Types

On line 19 of Listing 2.1, we see the function *addListener* takes an integer and a Listener object as parameters. This suggests that methods that take a *Listener*, like *List.add*, will be used. Any available object in the scope should increase the probability of calling a method that accepts the object as parameter.

Determining which variables are available is however a difficult task for the static analysis. Because of this, we approximate the available types by the parameter types of the enclosing method only. For lines 20-23 in Listing 2.1, this would be *int* and *org.eclipse.swt.widgets.Listener*.

Similar to the method name, this feature has similarities to the override context. Again, the same override context implies the same parameter types, but the same parameter types do not imply the same override context.

We will refer to this model as *parameters* or short *params*, where we see fit.

2.9 Overview

Table 2.1 shows an overview over the features presented in this section. It shows which features are set-valued, and which have a state space that is data dependent and grows with more available training data. As described in Section 1.5, set-valued features make a more complex model necessary. Many of the features have a value space that depends on the available training data. With more available data, this space becomes larger. With more free parameters, a model becomes more prone to overfitting, and takes up more memory. In the following we give an overview of the properties of the value space of the different features. We use a different order than in other parts of the section and Table 2.1, and order them in a way that expresses our expectation as to the size of the value space.

21

Table 2.1: Overview of the features

model	value space data-dependent	set-valued	similar to	prior work
calls		X		[Bru12]
override context	X		method name	[Bru12][Ama13]
definition kind			defining method	[Bru12]
defining method	X		definition kind	
method name	X	X	override context	
package name	X			
parameter types	X	X	override context	

Definition kind is in this sense a feature that comes almost for free: it has a value space that only contains 6 values, for every type, independent of the amount of training data. As we stated above, the actual values that appear for each type may in many cases just be a subset of those, reducing the value space even further.

Calls is set-valued, but its value space is only dependent on the type, not the amount of training data. Although calls needs a more complex model than, for example, definition kind, it still scales well because the model size in terms of memory does not depend on the amount of available data.

Defining method has a value space that potentially grows with more data, as there might be more methods that return the type. How much that space actually grows is dependent on the type. The more an instance of a type comes into scope through the definition kinds PARAMETER and METHOD_RETURN, the more this space will grow. Types that mostly come through NEW will also have a small value space for defining method, as there are only a few constructors per type. Overall, we expect the value space of defining method to grow gracefully for a lot of types. Also, it is not set-valued, as there is always exactly one definition for an object.

A package usually includes multiple types. While with growing amounts of data, the amount of seen package names will rise, we expect that it grows slower than the seen values of other features. Also, package name is not set-valued. On the other hand, we expect that there are only a few discriminative package names and a lot of noise. While we do not, in our implementation, do any value selection, we believe that the value space of package name could be considerably reduced by proper value selection.

Override context is not set-valued, but contains a value for every method that has been overridden in the training data. For types that are overridden, this includes typically more than one method. We expect the value space of this feature to be rather large.

Method name and parameter types can be seen as a more general form of override context. However, the generalization comes at the cost of being set-valued. We expect both to grow less quickly than override context, with parameter types growing slower than method name.

Chapter 3

Evaluation and Comparison of Base Models

In this section, we evaluate the base models, each of which is based on one of the features described in Section 2. In doing so, we want to answer the following questions:

1. Are the base models better than the frequency-baseline model?

2. How do the base models differ in predictive strength?

3. Is different context information useful for different types?

4. Is there one base model that is always better than the others?

Especially the last question is important to us. If we can show that there is not a base model that is always (meaning for every type) better, we would have shown a necessity for a type-dependent choice of base model or more complex models based on multiple features. We expect that the different features cover different, albeit correlated aspects, and thus that none of the base models is strictly better than the others. We also expect that for most types, there is not one single model that covers all relevant context information to correctly predict the expected methods; in Section 5 we evaluate more complex models to support this hypothesis.

24

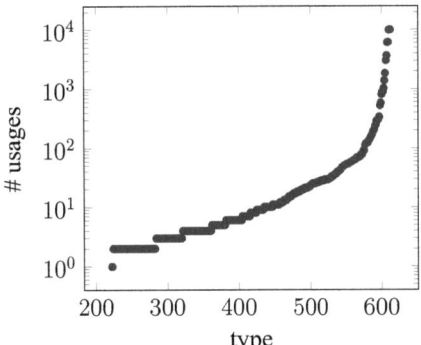

Figure 3.1: Usages of the types of the JRE in our evaluation data

3.1 Evaluation Data Set

We mine the class files of the Eclipse Kepler M6 build containing more than 4500 Eclipse plug-ins. At the time of writing, this exact data is no longer available through a public site. Additionally, we mined the Java 7 Runtime Library. Using this data provides us with a reasonable amount of example classes which are diverse with regard to used types and complexity, since Eclipse plug-ins range from UI classes over version-control systems to static-analysis software. Our features are extracted using a static analysis based on WALA[1].

We evaluate the base models of the classes of the JRE (Java Runtime Environment), mined from the usages in the libraries depicted above. The JRE is arguably used by almost every Java class in existence, therefore a model that predicts the JRE's methods well is valuable for most developers. According to [Blo], about half of the code completions that are triggered are triggered on JRE types. Heinemann et al. [HH11] also chose to evaluate the JRE type usages. A type usage, for us, is an occurrence of an object of this type in a method, when at least one method has been called on that type.

Figure 3.1 shows the amount of usage for each type of the JRE. We see that we do not have any data for approximately a third of the types. Another third was used

---

[1]http://wala.sourceforge.net/

Table 3.1: The 10 most used JRE classes

type	usages
java.lang.String	10000
java.lang.StringBuilder	10000
java.lang.StringBuffer	9872
java.util.Iterator	6161
java.util.List	6071
java.util.ArrayList	3635
java.util.Map	3011
java.util.HashMap	1833
java.lang.Class	1383
java.util.Set	1028

less than ten times. When plotting the data on a logarithmic scale both on the x- and y-axis, one can see the usages follow a Zipf distribution. This is similar to what can be observed in natural language, where there are also few words that are used a lot, while many words are only rarely used [MS99]. While the general trend was to be expected, we still find it interesting to find a distribution alike natural word frequencies in the artificial domain of source code and objects. A similar distribution has been observed for the SWT[2] classes [WKB09]. Since we expect the results for types with more usages to be more stable, we will only consider types for which we have more than 20 usages. We chose this number as we are still left with 126 types (about 20% of the total), and can still, with a ten-fold cross validation, mine each model from at least 18 usages.

Table 3.1 shows the top-10 types with regard to usages present in our evaluation data. We imposed a maximum of 10000 usages per type to reduce the load on our algorithms. We see that only *java.lang.String* and *java.lang.StringBuilder* were used more than 10000 times in our data. This hard-coded maximum does thus not bias our results for all other types. We expect that the results for String and StringBuilder are still representative and not severely biased.

---

[2]http://www.eclipse.org/swt/

3.2 Evaluation Scenario

For the evaluation, we chose to test with 50% of the calls observed, the other ones expected. We believe this covers the likely case that the programmer already has written something and then triggers the code completion. This is the same scenario that was used by [Bru12]. Of our base models, only the calls model uses the observed method calls. For all other models, this approach will lower the average ranking quality; already observed method calls are not expected by a test scenario as they belong to the context; on the other hand, models that don't take into account already called methods should propose the already called methods as they are obviously relevant in the surrounding context (or otherwise they would not have been used). This leads to highly ranked, not expected methods that lower the ranking metric.

We use a ten-fold cross validation to define the separation of training and test data. This means the data is separated in parts of 10% each; then, for each of these folds, the models are trained using the remaining 90% of data. The other 10% are used as test data. This is again as in [Bru12] and [Ama13].

For the parameter-types model, we selected 500 parameter types per type using the information gain criterion [Qui93]. We selected 100 method names per type for the method-name model. This choice is based on experimental results that we discuss in Section 3.4.

3.3 Evaluation Metric

For the comparison of the different models we use the average Normalized Discounted Cumulative Gain (avg. NDCG [JK02]) that is defined as:

$$DCG = \sum_i \frac{rel_i}{log_2(rank_i + 1)} \tag{3.1}$$

where rel_i is 1 if the method is expected, 0 otherwise

$$NDCG = \frac{DCG}{IDCG} \tag{3.2}$$

where IDCG is the ideal DCG

27

The ideal DCG is the one that would be achieved if the ranker ranked perfectly, meaning that the expected methods all appear at the top of the ranking.

This metric comes from a search-engine background, where it is assumed that the later a relevant document appears in the results, the less valuable it is for a user, since it takes more effort for the user to find [JK02]. The DCG metric tries to capture this by logarithmically discounting the value of a relevant document (or method in our case). The DCG metric is, however, not comparable when comparing rankings with different amounts of relevant documents. Since the number of methods that are used inside a method varies, we chose to use the normalized version of the DCG. This makes the metric comparable, but quite abstract. We still use it as it gives a single value describing the ranked list, and makes it easy to make qualitative statements.

We compare the different base models by their difference in average NDCG. This serves us well for plots, and gives us a general impression on the differences between the base models. We also use this in a qualitative way to help us make a decision whether one model is to be considered better than the other or not. We perform a paired, two-tailed t-test [She07] with a significance level of 5% to assert statistical significance of our qualitative statements. Through the t-test, we check for every type whether the difference of the two compared model's NDCG score is distributed with zero mean. If that is not the case, we can call the difference mean *statistically significant*. If we define $\overline{X}_D$ as the mean difference, s_D as the standard deviation of the differences, and n as the number of evaluation scenarios, the t-value can be computed as follows

$$t = \frac{\overline{X}_D}{s_D/\sqrt{n}} \tag{3.3}$$

This t-value, together with the number of evaluation scenarios, can be used to determine the statistical significance. Tables that can be used for this purpose can be found in [Com91]. Using a 5% significance level means that it is unlikely that the mean difference is a product of chance.

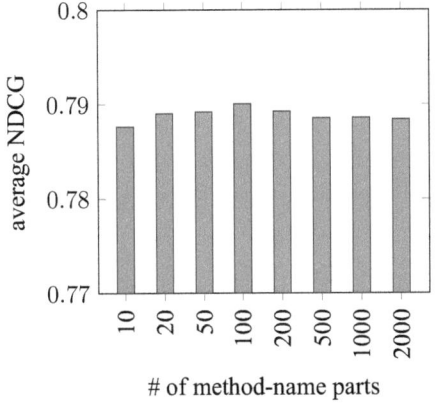

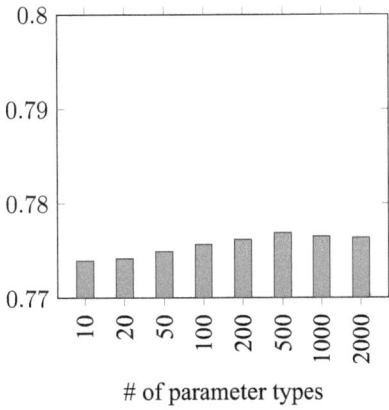

Figure 3.2: Results of the value selection experiment for method names

Figure 3.3: Results of the value selection experiment for parameter types

3.4 Results

In this section, we present the results of our evaluation. We start by discussing the value selection of the method-name and parameter-types models. We then answer the question whether the base models outperform the baseline model. Afterwards, we compare the different base models.

Figures 3.2 and 3.3 show the results of our value-selection experiment. The goal of this experiment was to find the number of values that maximize the performance of the method-names model and the parameter-types model, respectively. To do so, we averaged the NDCG over our complete evaluation data set, for different amounts of method-name parts and parameter types, respectively. As we said before, we selected the values through the Information Gain criterion [Qui93]. We argue that a maximum of the average NDCG should translate into maximal performance in our subsequent evaluation. Figure 3.2 shows that we found the maximum for the method-names model at 100 method-name parts. This is an interesting result, as it shows that relatively few method-name parts positively contribute to the ranking. On the other hand, Figure 3.3 shows that we found the maximum for the parameter-types model at 500 parameter types. This means that there are more parameter types that contribute to the final performance, but we can also already see that even with a handful of method-name parts, the method-name model already outperforms the parameter-types model.

Figure 3.4 shows a plot of the average NDCG values that the frequency model and the method-name model achieve for the different types of the Java Runtime Environment (JRE). We show the frequency model as blue line underlying the data points of the method-name model. For easier comparison, we sorted the values according to the NDCG of the frequency model. To additionally compare the performance to the amount of available training data, we add a green plot that shows the corresponding number of usages on a logarithmic scale.

To illustrate the plot, we marked the data point of the *java.util.LinkedHashMap* type; we can see that while the frequency model achieves an average NDCG of 0.56, the method-name model achieves 0.75. This means the rankings of the method-name model are better on average. In our data, some of the usages of this type are implementing LRU-Caches. Since all of them are implemented by subclassing *Linked-HashMap* and overriding *removeEldestEntry*, the method name is suitable for predicting that inside *removeEldestEntry*, the *size()* method is generally used. Similar to the just described data point, some data points are above the baseline, while others are below the baseline. A few of those are caused by implementation-dependent effects, like the *org.w3c.dom.Text* point we marked. In our data, two methods of that type generally appear in pairs, and receive the same scores by both models, but are returned in different order. This has an impact when a test scenario only asks for one of the methods.

Looking at the green plot (# usages), we see that the data exhibits no obvious correlation between the amount of training data and the performance of the models. This shows that the quality of a model depends stronger on how the API of that type looks like, than the amount of available data. Given a type, more data may mean better performance, but a type will not have better models than another type just by virtue of the amount of available data.

For comparing the base models, we are especially interested in the differences in the average NDCG scores between the different models. As in a diagram like Figure 3.4, the differences in NDCG are hard to see, we will in the following directly

30

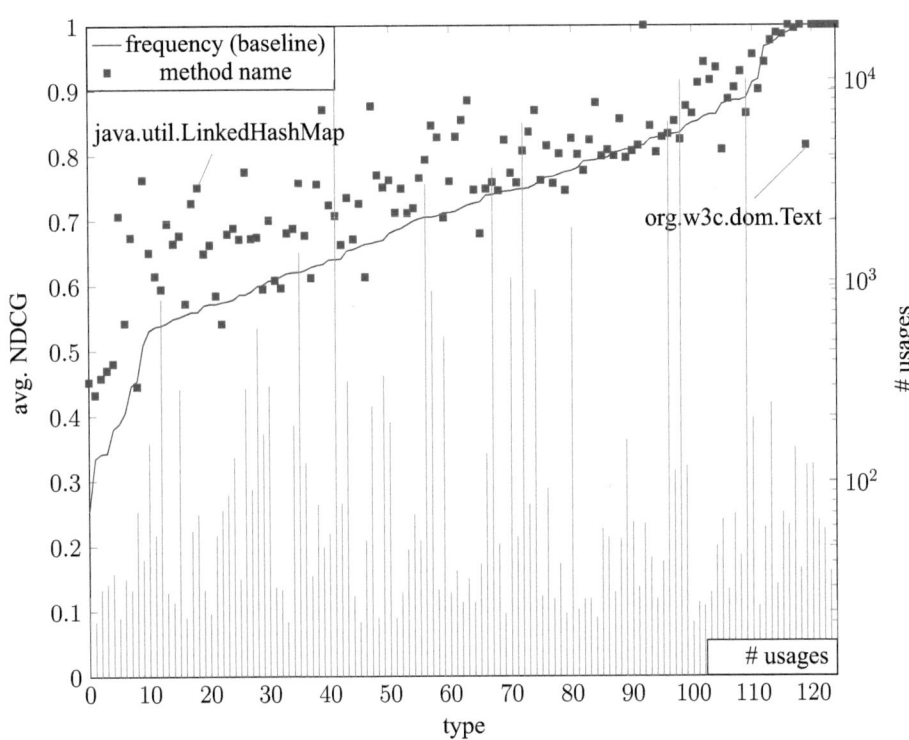

Figure 3.4: Avg. NDCG comparison of method-name model and frequency-based model, based on the JRE classes

visualize the differences of the NDCG.

Figure 3.5 shows the differences in the NDCG score between the base models and the frequency baseline. We again sort the data (this time by the NDCG difference) to make the plot easier readable. This way, the area between the plot and the x-axis can serve as visual indicator of the model's quality. The area above the x-axis indicates types for which the base model performed better than the baseline, while the area below the x-axis belongs to types for which the baseline was better. We can see that all models are better than the frequency baseline for most of the types, but perform worse for a few types. As shown in the example above, some of these instances are worse due to implementation-dependent effects, and we assume this is the case for some models that seem to perform better as well. The results still show a clear trend of the base models outperforming the frequency baseline.

An unexpected result is that the calls model outperforms the frequency baseline for 70 of the 126 types. This means that more than 50% of the types that are used often are typically used more than one time inside a method. We suppose this is slightly less due to the implementation-dependent effects discussed above; still, even if 40% of the types are typically used more than once in a method, this is more than we expected. We found that, of the remaining 56 types, calls only had an equal average NDCG score as the frequency baseline in 20 cases; we assume these were cases in which the calls model actually degenerated to the frequency baseline for all test scenarios of those types. For the remaining 36 types, the calls model performed worse, on average, than the baseline; this can be either due to overfitting, or due to implementation details as with *org.w3c.dom.Text* discussed above. If the call model failed due to overfitting for these types, this means that instances of those types are, at least sometimes, used more than once. Assuming that at least the 20% types for which the calls model performed equal to the baseline model are only used once typically, types that are used more than once make up 40-80% of all types, which is way above our expectations.

We want to answer the question whether one of the base models consistently outperforms all the others. If that was the case, we would not need to consider any other features than the one the best base model uses. Figure 3.6 shows a pairwise comparison of all the base models. In the following we will call the models that

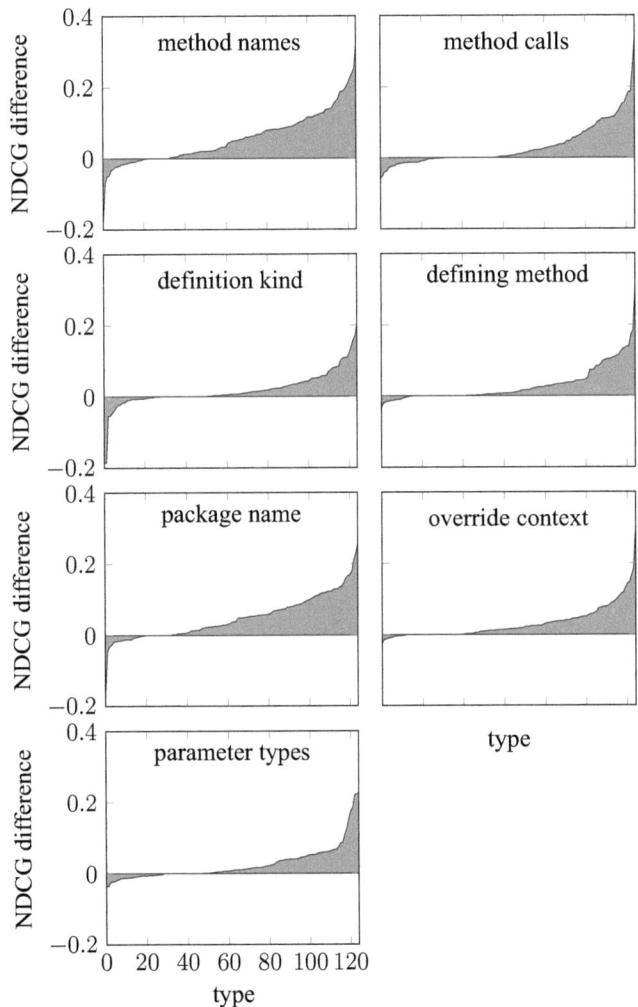

Figure 3.5: Avg. NDCG difference of the base models compared to the baseline for the JRE classes

appear on the columns *column models* and the models on the rows *row models*. The row models are used as the base for the comparison. Thus, area above the x-axis signifies types for which the column model is better, while area below the x-axis belongs to types where the row model is better. For example, the plot in the package column and kind row (marked in red) shows that the package model is better than the kind model for most types. We will now discuss the results with regard to the different models.

3.4.1 Calls

We now look at the calls column of Figure 3.6. We see that the calls model works well for about half the types, but cannot outperform the other models for the other types. The type *java.lang.Class*, as we stated in Section 2.2, is mostly used just once inside a given method. Consequently, the only model that does not outperform calls for this specific type is definition kind. On the other hand, the calls model is unbeaten for many of the *javax.swing.* * types. As those have to go through extensive initialization, multiple calls are typically done on instances of these types.

Table 3.2 shows a qualitative view on the data. It shows for each model for how many types calls was better, equal, or worse. The numbers inside parentheses denote how many of those were statistically significant. For example, calls achieved a higher average NDCG than context for 48 of the 126 types, for 23 of which the differences were statistically significant; context, on the other hand, achieved a higher NDCG for 61 types, of which the differences for 18 types were statistically significant. If we compare the models with regard to this qualitative measure, we see that calls is worse than all the other models, except kind.

If we take into account statistical significance, we can no longer say whether calls is worse, equal, or better than override context and params. This is because the statistical significance can tell us that it is unlikely that the performance difference for a type is caused by chance, but cannot tell us that two models perform equal for the type (or, in other words, that the difference is a consequence of chance).

This relatively bad performance was to be expected, seeing that the calls model was equal or worse than the baseline for 56 of the 126 types. Models that exploit

34

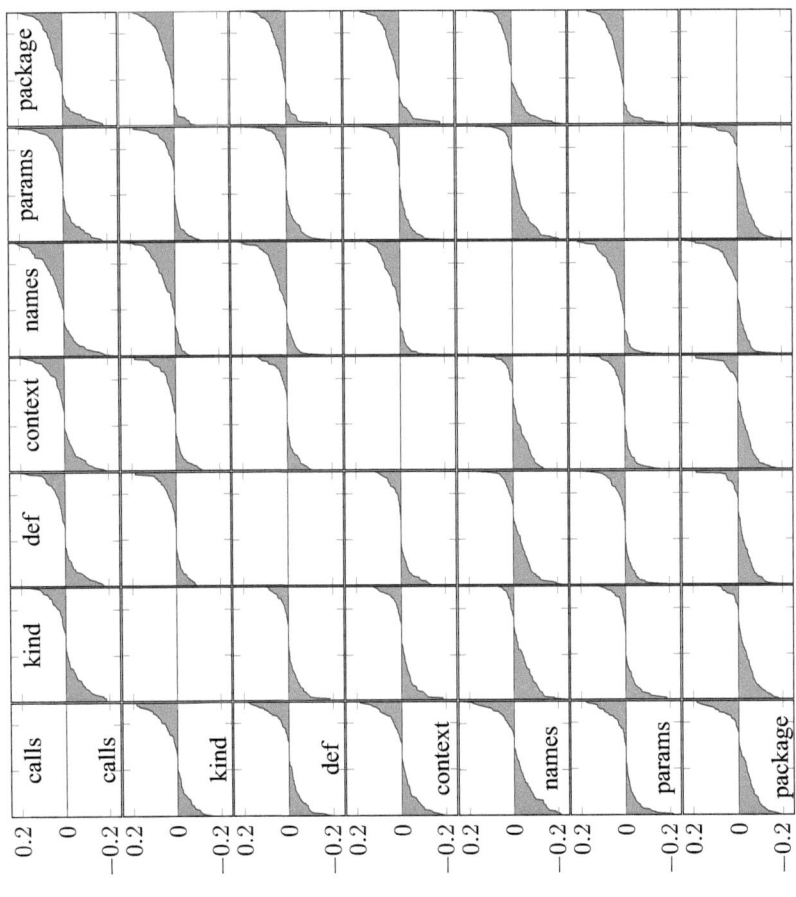

Figure 3.6: Avg. NDCG difference of the base models compared to the baseline for the JRE classes

35

Table 3.2: number of types for which calls performed better, equal, or worse than another model

model	calls		
	better (stat. signif.)	equal	worse (stat. signif.)
context	48 (23)	17	**61** (18)
kind	**60** (24)	14	52 (17)
def	44 (15)	21	**61** (18)
names	40 (11)	10	**76** (26)
package	36 (12)	12	**78** (33)
params	50 (17)	16	**60** (13)

context information apart from the calls benefit from types that are mostly just used once in a method. As stated above, there are less of such types than expected, but they still make up a significant portion of the total types. They also benefit from types that are sometimes used multiple times, but for which the common case is the single usage.

From Figure 3.6, we can see that for the types where calls works better than other models, it does so conceivably. On the other hand, the results for types for which the model does not work better also are conceivably worse. From Table 3.2, we take the information that the calls model performs equally well as the other models in only very few cases. We argue that these three facts show that calls is a feature that is mostly orthogonal to the other features, covering different aspects of a method's context than the other features.

3.4.2 Override context

Table 3.3 shows that the override-context model performed better than calls, kind, and params. It performed worse than def, names, and package. Taking into account statistical significance, we cannot even affirm anymore that it is better than calls .

Surprisingly, the override-context model performs better than params. Although, as we wrote in Section 2.6 and 2.8, names as well params can be seen as a more general version of override context, override context performs better than params, while at the same time being beaten by names for 79 of the 126 types. This indicates that

36

Table 3.3: number of types for which context performed better, equal, or worse than another model

model	context		
	better (stat. signif.)	equal	worse (stat. signif.)
calls	**61** (18)	17	48 (23)
kind	**66** (24)	14	46 (9)
def	46 (10)	25	**55** (11)
names	32 (4)	15	**79** (24)
package	31 (10)	16	**79** (26)
params	**61** (13)	14	51 (8)

params is overgeneralizing. Overgeneralization happens when too much valuable information is thrown away or aggregated in big classes. It can be seen as the opposite of overfitting, which happens when the model has so many free parameters that it can fit the training data very well, but fails on the testing data because it adapted too much on things that were specific to the training data. We discuss some of the reasons for the overgeneralization of params later in Section 3.4.7.

3.4.3 Definition kind

Table 3.4 again shows a qualitative comparison between definition kind and the other models. We conclude from this data that the definition-kind model was the least performant model overall. All other models perform better or equal to definition kind for more than half of the types. Still, no other model beats kind on every type. Looking at the kind column in Figure 3.6, we see however that even for the types where kind is better, it is not much better, compared to the differences that the other features exhibit among each other. Indeed, Table 3.4 shows that kind beats the other models in a statistically significant way for only a few types. As Figure 3.5 clearly tells us that definition kind is discriminative, this means there is stronger correlation between definition kind and the other features than there is pairwise correlation between the other features. Seeing the small state space of the definition-kind feature, this is not surprising, albeit unexpected.

On the other hand, we expected definition kind to be strongly correlated with

Table 3.4: number of types for which kind performed better, equal, or worse than another model

model	kind		
	better (stat. signif.)	equal	worse (stat. signif.)
calls	52 (17)	14	**60** (24)
context	46 (9)	14	**66** (24)
def	43 (12)	21	**61** (20)
names	33 (2)	11	**82** (28)
package	26 (3)	16	**84** (30)
params	53 (8)	19	54 (15)

defining method. It is unexpected that, although this seems to be the case, the correlation appears to be no stronger than the correlation to other features. We see however that there are at least 21 types (~1/6) for which kind and def performed equal. There are two possible reasons: Either both models degenerated to the frequency baseline in these cases, and were not discriminative at all, or they strongly correlated, to the point where both features described the same phenomena.

We found that both cases appear. In 17 of 21 cases, both models degenerated to the frequency baseline. One of these cases is the fourth-most used type *java.util.Iterator*. Iterator objects entered the scope in 5993 of 6161 cases (97.3%) as a METHOD_RETURN. From experience, we can assume almost all of these usages had the defining method of *java.util.Collection.iterator()*. That means that definition kind and defining method do not really provide any additional information about an Iterator object. One could also argue that the usage of an Iterator does not depend on the definition site, but is already determined by the API. All Iterators will have to call *next()*, almost all will call *hasNext()*, and some will call *remove()*. A similar case is *java.regex.Pattern*, which almost always enters a method through a call to *Pattern.compile()*. 18 of the 24 usages of *Pattern* have a definition kind of METHOD_RETURN. On the other hand, Pattern is a type on whose instances most of the time only one method is invoked. Most models will not be better than the baseline for such types. In fact, method name is the only model that improves upon the baseline for Pattern.

Table 3.5: number of types for which def performed better, equal, or worse than another model

model	def		
	better (stat. signif.)	equal	worse (stat. signif.)
calls	**61** (18)	21	44 (15)
context	**55** (11)	25	46 (10)
kind	**62** (20)	21	43 (12)
names	37 (7)	14	**75** (18)
package	30 (9)	15	**81** (27)
params	**59** (17)	16	51 (10)

3.4.4 Defining method

Table 3.5 shows that, from a qualitative standpoint, the only models that are better than the defining-method model are names and package. This is somewhat unexpected, as we considered the defining method to be among the less discriminative features. We are especially surprised to see from Figure 3.6 that there is a significant difference between the definition-kind model and defining method. As we stated in Section 2, we expected a considerable correlation between those two features. Instead, we now find that for many types, it is much more discriminative where the object comes from, than just knowing that it was constructed inside the surrounding method or was returned by some method invocation.

It is interesting to note that for calls, context and kind, there is a good amount of types where the models performed equally well (or bad). As we already discussed in the previous paragraph, this can be due to degeneration to the baseline for the same types, or by a strong correlation on this subset of types. In the same context, an object of such a type would always be created the same way, and the same calls would be invoked on that object. In 18 of 21 cases, the types where defining method is equal to calls are due to falling back to the frequency baseline. The same is true for 17 of the 21 cases for kind, and 17 of 25 cases for context. In total, defining method is equal to the frequency baseline for 25 types. This means that in a few cases, the models do indeed capture the same information, but for the most part, they are at least slightly different.

3.4.5 Method name

Method name is the second best model with regard to our qualitative measure. Table 3.6 shows that it performed better than every other model except package. Figure 3.6 shows a bigger area above the x-axis for names than for other models, which means that there are more types for which the method-name model is significantly better than there are types for which there is a big difference between other models. This is in agreement to the many types for which the names model is better in a statistically significant way, as can be seen in Table 3.6.

In Section 2.6, we argued that names can be seen as a more general feature than override context. We expected the names model to perform better because of better generalization. As we can see from Table 3.6, this expectation was met. Names performed better than context for almost two third of the types.

From Figure 3.2, we see that even with only few method-name parts, we can achieve good results overall. This was surprising. When looking at the models, we found the following facts that help us understand the correlation between method names and method calls:

- Of all instances in which *List.toArray()* was called, 12% happened in methods that contain the word "selected", and 8 % in methods that contain the term "to".

- Of all instances in which *List.get(int)* was called (almost half of the usages), 13 % were in methods that contain "spec". We discuss this further below.

- Of all instances in which *Iterator.next()* was called, about 15% occurred in methods that contain "get". Also interesting: Only 80% of Iterator uses called *next()*.

- Of all instances in which *String.replaceFirst()* was called, 75% occurred in methods that contain "get".

Especially the *List.get(int)* case reveals a problem of the method-names model. Almost all usages actually come from the same project Photran[3], which provides tool support for the Fortran language inside Eclipse. Most of these usages come

---

[3]http://www.eclipse.org/photran/

40

Table 3.6: number of types for which names performed better, equal, or worse than another model

model	names		
	better (stat. signif.)	equal	worse (stat. signif.)
calls	**76** (26)	10	40 (11)
context	**79** (24)	15	32 (4)
kind	**82** (28)	11	33 (2)
def	**75** (18)	14	37 (7)
package	48 (15)	16	**62** (9)
params	**86** (27)	14	26 (6)

from the Fortran parser. We suspect a lot of this code is generated. Even if this is not the case, it shows that not respecting project boundaries during the folding process actually benefits models like method names, since there is often a project-wide naming convention that does not reflect the global method naming behavior. To be precise, this is not so much a problem of the model, but a problem of our evaluation setup. We will discuss this further in Section 3.6.

3.4.6 Package name

From Table 3.8, we see that the package name works surprisingly well for almost two thirds of the 126 types we evaluated. In that sense, it was the best model in our evaluation. In Section 2.7, we expressed our expectation that the package name carries less context information than the other features. Looking at the package column in Figure 3.6, we see that package had a significantly higher NDCG score than the other models, and the Table 3.8 shows this is statistically significant in many cases.

We conclude that the package name conveys more context information than we initially expected. On the other hand, this might be an effect of our evaluation setup. Since our folding strategy was allowed to put data from the same project and even the same class file in different folds, it is possible that we have a bias here. We cannot be certain that it is actually the package name itself that is discriminative. Maybe we just showed that method calls within the same project or class file correlate strongly. Since we find the great result of package surprising, future work should

Table 3.7: number of types for which package performed better, equal, or worse than another model

model	package		
	better (stat. signif.)	equal	worse (stat. signif.)
calls	**78** (33)	12	36 (12)
context	**79** (26)	16	31 (10)
kind	**84** (30)	16	26 (3)
def	**81** (27)	15	30 (9)
names	**62** (9)	16	48 (15)
params	**86** (33)	16	24 (3)

further investigate this feature to assert its utility.

3.4.7 Parameter types

As can be seen in Table 3.8, parameter types performed worse than most other models, except calls and kind. We expected it to perform better. We argue that this result comes from two observations:

On the one hand, we argue that there is an abundance of parameterless methods. Inside the scope of a parameterless method, the parameter-types model will degenerate to the frequency model. Also, the prediction of parameterless methods does not benefit as much from the context information of available types as the prediction of methods that take arguments. We have seen that there are a lot of types for which the method calls do not strongly correlate, leading to a bad performance of the calls model. In the absence of correlation to methods that need arguments, parameterless methods will not benefit from knowing which types are available in the current scope.

On the other hand, many objects do not enter a method's scope through the parameters. Apart from this being the whole point of the definition-kind and defining-method feature, an example of this is *java.util.List*. Of the 6071 usages of List in our data, only in 2851 cases did the object enter the method's scope through the parameter list. We conclude that for many types, the approximation of the available types through the parameter types is too crude and insufficient to produce good models.

The model is still useful for some types. In fact, Table 3.8 shows that it wins in

Table 3.8: number of types for which params performed better, equal, or worse than another model

model	params		
	better (stat. signif.)	equal	worse (stat. signif.)
calls	**59** (12)	17	50 (18)
context	51 (7)	15	**60** (15)
kind	49 (19)	20	57 (6)
def	49 (10)	19	**58** (14)
names	26 (6)	14	**86** (27)
package	24 (3)	16	**86** (33)

direct comparison to calls, if we leave statistical significance aside. This is again an indicator of the multitude of types that are typically just used once inside a method. On the other hand, we said before that calls is better than kind, while Table 3.8 shows kind is equal to params. This is an interesting situation that only appears for these three models. We conclude from this loop that kind was better than params for at least some of the types where calls was better than both models. If we only consider the statistically significant differences, then params is actually better than kind, and incomparable to calls.

3.5 Model Size

One motivation for using simpler models is a reduced model size in terms of free parameters and thus a smaller memory footprint. Smaller models mean, for a code-completion engine, not only less memory consumption at runtime, but also reduced loading time, which is a significant factor for the user experience. A code-completion engine that takes several seconds every time a new model needs to be loaded is not preferable.

We have two different types of models, as described in Section 1.5. Features that assume exclusive values - such as override context, defining method, definition kind, and package name - can be modeled as depicted in Figure 1.5. These only require the conditional probabilities $p(\text{method}|\text{feature})$.

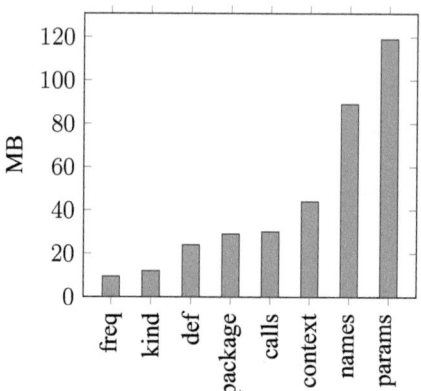

Figure 3.7: Aggregated model size of the JRE types, for the different base models

Table 3.9: Model types

model	type
calls	set-valued
kind	exclusive
context	exclusive
def	exclusive
names	set-valued
package	exclusive
params	set-valued

Set-valued features, however, need the more complex model depicted in Figure 1.6. Such a model has a significantly higher memory consumption as there are more free parameters. Set-valued features are calls, method names, and parameter types.

We store our models as serialized Java objects. We argue that the size of a model in this format directly correlates with the number of free parameters and is thus suited for comparison of the models with regard to complexity and memory consumption. Figure 3.7 shows a bar plot of the aggregated memory consumption of all JRE model instances for the different base models.

As we can see from Figure 3.7, the more complex models like method names and parameter types take up considerable amounts of memory, also due to their large state space. Calls, which is also set-valued, does not take up as much memory as the state space is independent of the amount of training data, and thus limited. As expected, the frequency model takes up an order of magnitude less space than the biggest models.

It is interesting to note the difference between def, context, and package. We clearly see that, on average, there are less defining methods than there are package names. On the other hand, there are less individual package names than there are override contexts. This is more or less in accordance with our expectations stated in Section 2.9.

Seeing that the parameter-types model had such a bad performance in our evaluation, compared to other models, and that the model takes up more space than three of the smaller models together, we conclude that it is not worth the memory.

Despite what we said in Section 2.9 about the size of state spaces, the override-context model takes up less space than the parameter-types and method-names model. This is because of an inherent difference: While the override context has always one exclusive value in a scenario, parameter types and method names are actually set-valued features. As described above and in Section 1.5, this makes a considerably more complex model necessary.

3.6   Threats to Validity

In this section, we discuss potential threats to the validity of our evaluation. Identifying such threats is important to validate the plausibility of our observations and conclusions. It also reveals potential future work to be done.

One major part that influences the results is the chosen data set. Future work may reveal that usages of the JRE types are not representative for types outside the JRE. This influences especially the comparison between the models. It is possible that GUI-Frameworks like SWT are better modeled by exploiting the override context than, for example, the package name. The evaluation of a representative data set should mirror what kind of types the developers trigger code completion on, while they develop. We believe that the JRE is representative. It contains the GUI-Framework Swing, classes for networking, IO, collections, etc. It is used frequently

45

by developers. We have no data that tells us how much JRE types are used compared to the types of other libraries, but we expect them to be the most frequently used.

The other part is the client libraries that we mined the usages of the JRE types from. Although our evaluation data consists of hundreds of diverse projects, split up in 4500 Eclipse plug-ins, we need to ask the question whether Eclipse plug-ins or the Eclipse projects are representative users of the JRE types. For example, *java.lang.Class* is the ninth most used type of the JRE in our evaluation data. We doubt that *Class* is such a frequently used type in other contexts. Nevertheless, we believe that our data set is, for the most part, representative and thus suited for evaluation.

While our data set consisted of hundreds of different projects, split up in 4500 Eclipse plug-ins, we still found that there are only few types that are frequently used. Of course any system that learns from data is threatened by a lack of training data. The number of 20 usages that we set as minimum for our evaluation may be too small - after all, rarely used types are rarely used, the need for good models is smaller. We used Figure 3.4 to argue that there is no direct correlation between the number of usages for a type and the quality of its model. However, given a type, one can expect to see a difference in model quality with changing amount of training data. With more data, we might see that the models for certain types become far better. Also, while models with few parameters like definition kind and calls may not be especially sensitive to the amount of training data, other models like method name and parameter types may benefit much more from more training data. We might find that, given enough training data, parameter types becomes one of the best models.

Our evaluation scenario left 50% of the used method calls as context. We needed that to be able to compare to the calls model. This biases the evaluation, however. The first problem is that it is unclear how representative this scenario really is. The second problem is that this approach favors the calls model and limits the maximally possible performance of the other models. The third problem is that it makes the other models sensitive to the order in which they propose the methods that originally were present. It is correct for those models to propose all of the originally present methods, but only 50% are actually expected by the evaluation scenario. The expected methods are randomly selected in our evaluation setup. Assume there is a type X with two

46

methods *X.a()* and *X.b()*. In a method that uses both, one model ranks *a()* first and *b()* second, and an other model ranks *b()* first and *a()* second. Which one of the models is considered "better" by our evaluation now depends on the random choice of the implementation whether *a()* belongs to the context and *b()* is expected or the other way around. In reality however, they have both proposed the correct methods, given the context information they know. We have actually observed this problem with *org.w3c.dom.Text*, as described in Section 3.4. We argue, however, that this problem should become smaller with more data, as fewer methods will have equal scores in a given context, and random effects will be averaged out.

We did not respect project boundaries during our folding procedure. As we said in Section 3.4.5, this favors models that can exploit project naming conventions like method names and package names. Also, it introduces another possible bias. We saw that about half of the *java.util.List* usages actually come from the same project. Cutting off the usages after a certain maximum actually makes this bias even worse. Projects that have a bigger code base also favor models that work good for them, while smaller projects have less influence. Although one might argue that weighting bigger projects more is in favor of representativeness, this is a problem as project-specific patterns can strongly influence the evaluated models. Generated code, which almost automatically leads to a big code base, is very regular and is arguably not really representative when it comes to the way a human developer would write code. Heuristics to discern machine-generated from humanly-generated code in Java could be (i) the synthetic modifier, which is meant to be used for generated code, (ii) annotations like *javax.annotation.Generated*, and (iii) heuristics like scanning the class hierarchy for cues to commonly used parser generators like ANTLR[4]. Heinemann et al. [HH11], whose work was also based on identifiers (and thus should exhibit similar problems due to project-specifics), evaluated both Cross Project Recommendation (training data not from the same project as the test data) and Intra Project Recommendation (training data only from the same project as the test data). Their work confirms that usages are more similar inside a single project than across project boundaries. Whether or not this is a threat to our evaluation depends on the goal: If the anticipated scenario is a single developer (or developer team) that trains his

---

[4]www.antlr.org/

personal code completion assistant to help him save as much keystrokes as possible, then exploiting such correlations is good and desirable. If the goal is to share and distribute knowledge of unknown APIs between different developers and projects, exploiting such correlations is dangerously close to the overfitting one would like to avoid. In this thesis, although we favor the collaborative viewpoint, we never assumed one specific position. Thus our evaluation is not devalued, but seeing that these correlations seemingly outperform any other context information is an actual result.

3.7 Conclusion

In this section, we saw that the proposed features from Section 2 are discriminative in the sense that they perform better than the frequency baseline. We performed a qualitative comparison of the base models, showing that some models are actually better than others, on average.

Figure 3.8 shows a summary of these qualitative results, and how they result in a partial order between the models. As the comparison between params on the one hand, and calls and kind on the other hand was unclear, we chose to see them as uncomparable for the purpose of this figure. As the figure only shows a summary of the qualitative result, this partial order is however not to be seen as an answer to question 4, whether one model is better than all the others for all types.

We have shown that the package name is a very good feature for code completion. We argue however, that it is not suited for cross-project recommendations, and that the results especially show that there are big intra-project correlations. Exploiting these correlations is useful in a scenario where a developer feeds his own usages into the system and has been done by Robbes et al. [RL08] and Heinemann et al. [HH11]. However, when the focus is on sharing knowledge between developers and projects, as in the works of Marcel Bruch [Bru12] and Sven Amann [Ama13], exploiting those correlations comes very close to the overfitting one would actually like to avoid.

Although our qualitative comparison between the different base models showed that some features are, on average, better than others, we have also seen that no model outperforms any of the other models for all 126 types that we evaluated. When com-

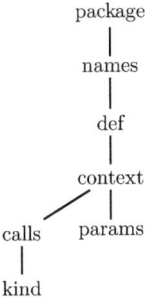

Figure 3.8: Partial order relation between the base models (higher means better, params is not comparable to calls and kind)

paring the base models, we found that every one of them is better than the others for at least 20% of the types. This clearly shows there is not one feature that perfectly explains the called methods. Rather, they describe different aspects that are all needed for a good prediction.

Our approach, that we describe in the subsequent sections, is to combine the base models to form an ensemble model, instead of creating one big model that contains all the features. We do so to reduce the necessary parameters and achieve a good generalization, compared to such a big model.

Chapter 4

Ensembles

Using classifiers based on only one feature or one family of features is problematic: First of all, using more features has the potential to improve predictions. After all, different features are good for different types. Second, if features are missing - for example if there are no method calls given - then a classifier relying only on this feature will degrade very quickly. Using more features in a single model however can be prone to overfitting, as there are more free parameters. To be feasible, one needs to stick with reasonable conditional independence assumptions like we already did. Therefore we experiment with ensembles that preserve these assumptions.

We focus on creating ensemble rankers through a type-dependent linear combination of the base models, as shown in Equation 4.1. This captures our intention that for different types, different base models are more "trustworthy" than others.

$$f(x|ctx) = \sum_{model} w_{model} * f_{model}(x|ctx) \tag{4.1}$$

We can further reduce the space of w to the standard simplex (described by Equations 4.2 and 4.3), as the scale of w does not change the ordering of the x's, and the non-negativity of the weights leads to non-negative scores. Restricting the possible values of w to a compact set like the standard simplex is also important to guarantee the existence of an optimal solution to our problem.

$$\sum_i w_i = 1 \tag{4.2}$$

$$w \geq 0 \tag{4.3}$$

Both constraints together also have the additional benefit that, if all f_{model} are conditional probability distributions, then f is a conditional probability distribution as well.

For training the ensemble, we first need to decide upon an error measure that we want to minimize. First, we formulate our problem, and relaxations of the problem. We also discuss whether the starting formulation really is the one that is appropriate for our intention.

By training the code recommendation model, we would ideally want that the item that the developer actually wants is the one that has the highest rank. We can therefore use our training data to formulate the following optimization problem with linear constraints.

$$\underset{w}{\text{minimize}} \quad 0$$

subject to

$$w^T f(x_{expct(i)}; ctx_i) \geq w^T f(x_j; ctx_i), \ i = 1, \ldots, n, j = 1, \ldots, m_i.$$

$$\sum_i w_i = 1$$

$$w \geq 0$$

$$\tag{4.4}$$

This captures our intention in the sense that if there is a solution to this problem, it will perfectly rank in the training scenarios. We always need to keep in mind though, that this does not mean it will also perfectly rank in other scenarios. Also, this formulation is likely to not have a solution at all, for example if all base classifiers agree on a wrong prediction in one scenario. Therefore we need to relaxate this formulation.

4.1 Linear Relaxation

To ensure the existence of a solution to problem 4.4, we use the following relaxation, by introducing slack variables:

$$\underset{w,\xi}{\text{minimize}} \quad \sum_{i=1,\dots,n,j=1,\dots,m_i} \xi_{ij}$$

subject to

$$w^T f(x_j; ctx_i) - w^T f(x_{expct(i)}; ctx_i) = \xi_{ij}, \ i = 1, \dots, n, j = 1, \dots, m_i$$

$$\sum_i w_i = 1$$

$$w \geq 0$$

$$(4.5)$$

We choose to use a linear loss instead of a 0/1-loss because we hope for better generalization by rewarding weight vectors that increase the difference between expected items and the other ones.

Problem 4.5 is equivalent to

$$\underset{w}{\text{minimize}} \quad w^T \left(\sum_{i=1,\dots,n,j=1,\dots,m_i} f(x_j; ctx_i) - f(x_{expct(i)}; ctx_i) \right)$$

subject to

$$\sum_i w_i = 1$$

$$w \geq 0$$

$$(4.6)$$

We will refer to the resulting ensemble model as *linear ensemble*. This is a linear problem easily solvable with the simplex algorithm. As we said in Section 1.6.2, the simplex algorithm always returns solutions in the corners of the feasible region. The corners of the feasible region of Problem 4.6 are the unit vectors. Using this formulation, we would therefore always give weight 1 to the classifier that is best according to our error function. This is bad because (i) choosing exactly one classifier is surely overfitting, and (ii) the error function is not the same as the one we are going to evaluate.

To avoid always giving the whole weight to one of the base models, we thus need a non-linear objective function.

4.2 Exponential Error

Based on problem 4.6, we formulate our optimization problem by using an exponential error instead of a linear. We will call the resulting ensemble model *exponential ensemble*.

$$
\begin{aligned}
&\underset{w}{\text{minimize}} && \sum_{i=1,\dots,n,\, j=1,\dots,m_i} e^{w^T(f(x_j;ctx_i)-f(x_{expct(i)};ctx_i))} \\
&\text{subject to} \\
&&& \sum_i w_i = 1 \\
&&& w \geq 0
\end{aligned}
\tag{4.7}
$$

Using an exponential error means we deem it far worse if the expected type is far away from the first position, but don't rate it as positive if the rating of the expected item is much higher than the others.

4.3 L2-Regularization

Using the exponential error still favors extreme weight values. Extreme values are problematic because they can induce overfitting. One common form of regularization is L2-Regularization [Bis06]. This regularization adds the sum of squares of the weights, or in other words, the square of the weight vector's L2-Norm, as additional term to the objective function. This favors weight factors that are closer to the middle of the feasible region described by equations 4.2 and 4.3, and thus avoids extreme weights. We will call the resulting ensemble model the *regularized ensemble*.

$$\underset{w}{\text{minimize}} \quad ||w||_2^2 + C * \left(\sum_{i=1,\dots,n,j=1,\dots,m_i} e^{w^T(f(x_j;ctx_i)-f(x_{expct(i)};ctx_i))} \right)$$

subject to

$$\sum_i w_i = 1$$

$$w \geq 0$$

where   C is a weighting factor that trades off between weight norm and error

$$(4.8)$$

To be able to trade-off between the error and the regularization, Problem 4.8 includes a free parameter C, which allows giving more or less weight to the error and thus either stress the regularization more or give priority to a small training error.

4.4   Model averaging

Taking the regularization to the extreme, we also want to evaluate how averaging the scores of the different models behaves. We expect this to perform worse than a more elaborate model, but we want this approach to serve as a baseline for the ensemble models. For the sake of this thesis, we will refer to the resulting model as *averaged ensemble*.

$$p_{\text{ensemble}}(\text{method}|\text{context}) = \sum_{i=1}^{n} \frac{p_{\text{model}_i}(\text{method}|\text{context})}{n} \qquad (4.9)$$

This is similar to *bootstrap aggregation* that averages different versions of the same model trained on slightly different data [Bis06]. The same arguments that are used in [Bis06] to argue that the expected error of the averaged model decreases with respect to the original model also apply here. For uncorrelated errors, the expected sum-of-squares error of an averaged ensemble is reduced proportionally to the number of members in the ensemble, wrt. the average error of those members. Since this property only fully holds for uncorrelated errors, bootstrap aggregation tries to solve this by training the members of the ensembles on different data. We, on the other hand, use the same data but inherently different models.

While we showed in Section 3.4 that there is correlation between some of the features to a certain degree, we also showed that the base models are, for the most types, different. We can thus expect that an averaged ensemble will better predict the method's scores and thus produce a better ranking than the base models.

We expect that the averaged ensemble will have a less varying performance, albeit we don't expect it to beat the base models for the types where the base models are especially good. Compared to the other models, we expect this simple approach to not beat the more complicated ones, especially the exponential ensemble.

Chapter 5

Evaluation of Ensembles

In this section we evaluate the models that result from applying the methods discussed in Section 4. We use the same data set that we used for evaluating the base models (see Section 3) and the same evaluation scenarios. We use every base model as component of our ensembles, to get an idea of their value as ensemble member. As with the base models, we first check that the ensembles outperform the frequency baseline. Then we compare them to the base models to see whether the ensembles outperform the base models. The motivation for creating ensemble models is the hope that they will outperform the base models in most cases, due to the additional context information they are able to use.

Thus we are interested in essentially the same questions as we were for the base models:

1. Should weights be type-dependent?

2. Do the ensemble models outperform the frequency baseline?

3. Do the ensembles outperform the base models?

4. Do the more complex ensembles outperform the averaged model?

5. Which optimization problem produces the best ensemble among our three problems?

We expect that our evaluation will confirm that weights should be type-dependent. This is because the base models themselves performed differently well on different

56

types. We concluded in Section 3.7 that there is not one base model that suits every type. In this section we expect that there is also not a subset of the base models that fit every type. Observing type-dependent weights that favor different models for different types would confirm this. This thesis would be falsified if there was an ensemble that consistently outperforms all base models, but never gives any weight to one specific base model.

Type-independent weights, on the other hand, would have the benefit that types for which there are only few examples could, at least for the weighting of the base models, benefit from the examples of more common types.

5.1   Optimization of the C parameter of the L2-regularized model

The L2-regularized ensemble has a free variable in its optimization problem used to compute the weights (Problem 4.8): The free variable C trades-off between regularization and error reduction. The other ensembles do not have such a free parameter.

The first thing we need to do for our evaluation is optimizing the free variable C. We experimented with a wide range of values for C over 8 orders of magnitude, namely 10^{-4} to 10^3. Figure 5.1 shows the average NDCG over the whole data set for different values of C. We see that we found a - potentially local - maximum at $C = 0.01$. We also see the method is not overly sensitive to the values of C, at least in the value range we investigated. For all C values that we examined, the average NDCG score was between 0.8085 and 0.8095. We therefore set the C value to a fixed 0.01 for the remainder of our evaluation.

Although we determined C in a type-independent way, we think it should be dependent on the amount of available training data, and thus type-dependent. Since the amount of training data directly influences the size of the summed error term, but the weight vector's L2-Norm always stays within the interval $[0, 1]$, more training data should mean smaller C.

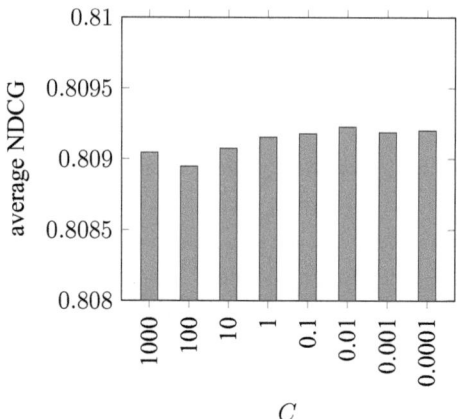

Figure 5.1: Results of the C parameter selection experiment for the L2-regularized ensemble

5.2 Comparison to frequency baseline

In this section we will compare the ensemble models to the frequency baseline. This allows us to answer question 2, whether the ensembles outperform the frequency baseline. Failing to do so would imply overfitting that is introduced through combining the base models. Our expectation, however, is that the ensembles beat the baseline as the base models do.

Figure 5.2 shows that, indeed, the ensemble models all beat the frequency baseline. It is interesting to see that for some types, the frequency baseline is again better. This is in part due to the fact that the base models themselves are worse than the baseline for some types and in part because our optimization algorithm fails to find a solution before hitting a stopping criterion. Failing to train a model results in a zero average NDCG score, as we defined no fallback mechanism.

A reason for failing to optimize is that the quadratic penalty method that we use (see Section 1.6.3) stops after a certain amount of attempts to find a feasible optimum. This amount may not be enough in some cases. Two exemplary cases for which the exponential ensemble did not produce any models was *java.io.PrintStream* and *javax.swing.JPanel*.

58

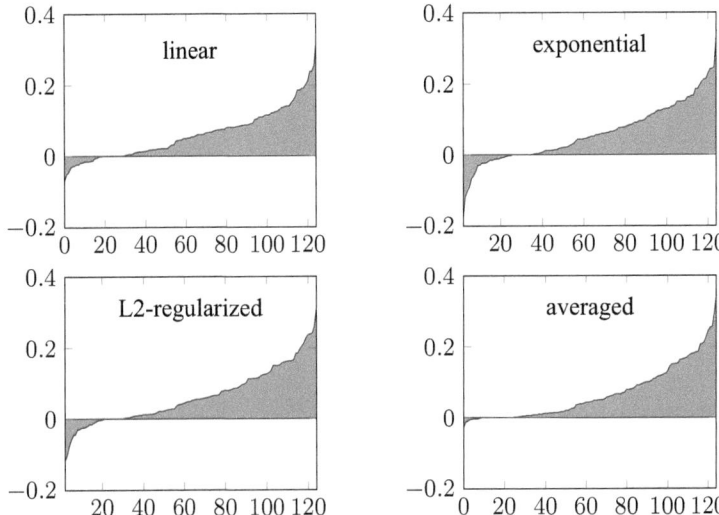

Figure 5.2: Normalized discounted cumulative gain for the JRE classes, compared to the frequency baseline

Interesting to note here is the linear ensemble, which for most of the types chose the method names model as the one to give the full weight to. If we compare Figure 5.2 with Figure 3.4, we see that the simple linear objective function was able to catch at least one type for which the method names model performed bad, and chose a different model for this type.

Our expectation that averaging the base models gets rid of many mistakes of the base models is met: Figure 5.2 shows that the averaged ensemble is better or equal than the baseline for 115 of 126 types, and only slightly worse for the remaining 9 types. No other model in our evaluation, base model or ensemble, managed to outperform the baseline on such a consistent base. The linear ensemble beat the baseline for 106 types, the exponential ensemble for 100 types, and the regularized ensemble for 105 types.

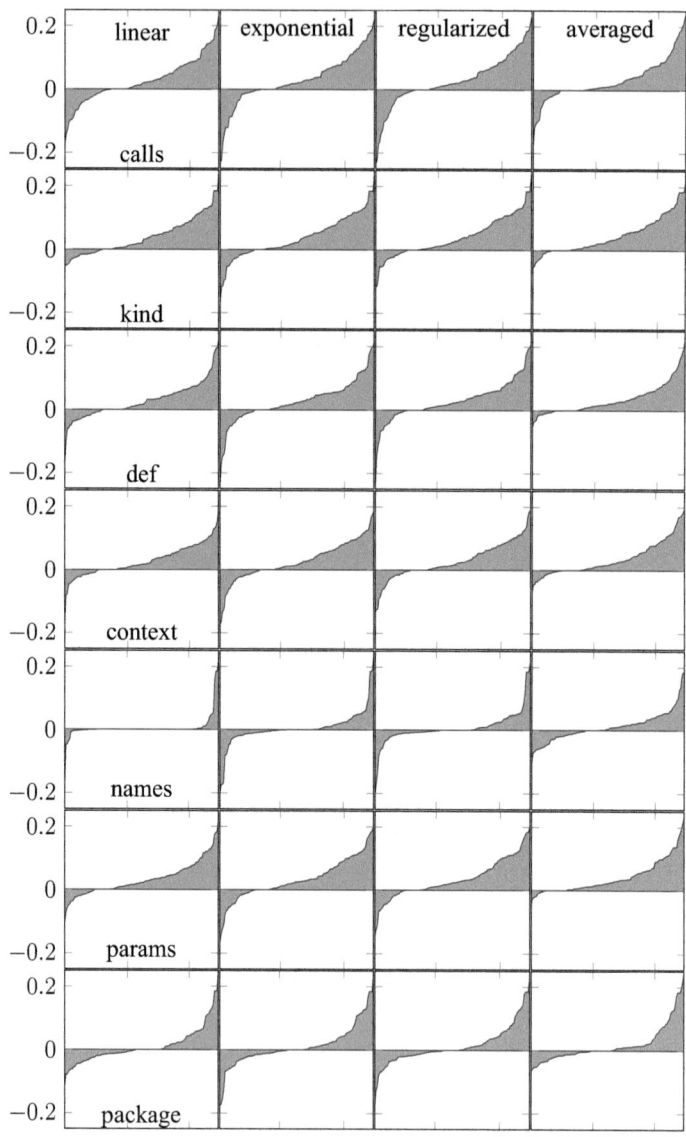

Figure 5.3: Comparison of ensembles and base models

5.3 Comparison to base models

Figure 5.3 shows a comparison between the ensemble models and the base models, similar to the comparison between the base models in Section 3.4. We again compare the differences in NDCG for the various types of our evaluation data set. We want to answer question 3, whether exploiting multiple types of context information by combining the base models makes the predictions better.

From the comparison in Figure 5.3, we can see that all ensembles outperformed the base models on average, but not for all types. This is in part due to the fact that the ensembles gave a lot of weight to the names model for most types. The linear ensemble, for example, chose to give all weight to the names model for most types, which we see in Figure 5.3 if we look at the linear column and names row. There we see that for almost all types, the linear model performed equal to the names model, which means that the name model got all the weight. Since the names model already performed so well in the comparison with the other base models, it is not surprising that ensembles that give a lot of weight to the names model will perform better than or equal to the other base models for most types.

The averaged ensemble again performs very well. In the averaged column in Figure 5.3 is shown that for all base models except names and package, the averaged ensemble showed equal or better performance for more than 100 types. Only the package-name model comes close to this result, but none of the other base models had such a consistently good result. Names beat the averaged ensemble for 44 types, package for 49 types. They thus beat the averaged ensemble less often than they beat any of the other base models. This again shows that one base model alone is not enough to fully cover the relevant context information that is discriminative for a type.

5.4 Comparison to averaged ensemble

We now compare the different ensemble models to the averaged ensemble, which we see as baseline. This helps us to answer two of our questions from the beginning:

Do the more complex ensembles outperform the averaged ensemble and should

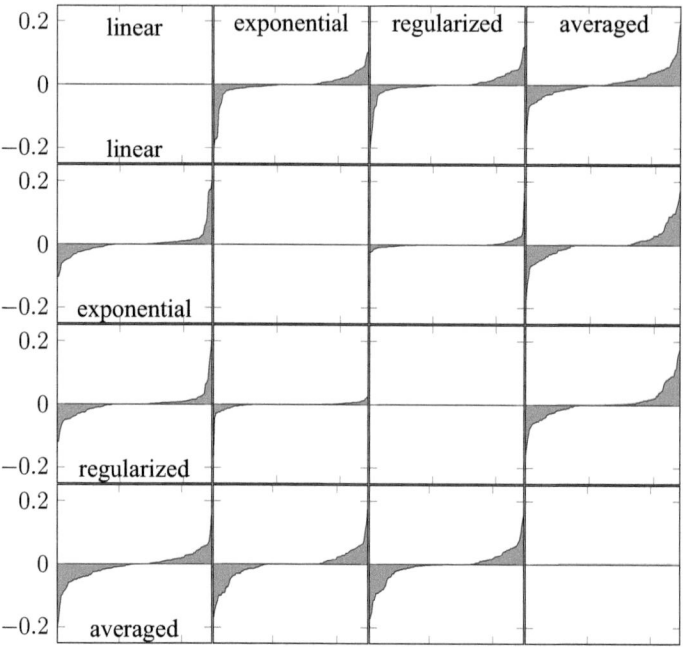

Figure 5.4: Comparison of the different ensembles

weights be type-dependent? If the other ensemble models outperformed the aver-aged ensemble for some types, then we would see that at least the type-independent approach of assigning equal weight to all base models is not optimal. On the other hand, if the averaged ensemble proved to be better than the other approaches for *all* types, then we would need to revisit the question whether type-independent weights could be optimal after all.

One conclusion we can draw from the comparison of the ensemble models to the base models in Figure 5.3 is that the averaged ensemble, although it also does not beat the base models for every type, has less types than the other ensembles for which the base models are actually better. This translates into Table 5.1 showing that the averaged ensemble is better than the other models for a significant amount of types, namely 62 for the linear model, 61 for the exponential model, and 67 for

Table 5.1: number of types for which the averaged ensemble performed better, equal or worse than another ensemble

| | averaged | | |
model	better (stat. signif.)	equal	worse (stat. signif.)
linear	62 (18)	14	50 (9)
exponential	61 (9)	10	55 (9)
regularized	67 (9)	14	45 (7)

the regularized model. However, it does not beat the other ensembles for every type. In fact, the averaged column in Figure 5.4 shows that the differences between the averaged model are substantial both in the positive and the negative direction. This shows that performance is sensitive to the weighting, and different types benefit from different weighting. Although we cannot answer the question whether weight should be type-dependent or type-independent conclusively, we see this result as a support for our thesis that weights should be type-dependent.

That the averaged ensemble performed the best of our approaches is unexpected, and shows that our optimization problems do not optimize the right thing. The averaged model performs better than all base models on themselves. It is also interesting that the exponential model actually chose to evenly distribute the weight as well for the 10 most used types (see Table 3.1 for a list), which means there was a local minimum or a saddle point of the error function at that point. Assuming there was a local minimum, this shows that the different features are all important for those types, albeit not necessarily in all scenarios. One could argue that this shows that in the limit, every type should benefit equally well from the different base models, which is an assumption in favor of type-independent weights. On the other hand, Figure 5.4 clearly shows that for there are types that would benefit from a different weight distribution. This again strengthens our thesis that weighting should be type-dependent.

5.5 Conclusion

We conclude that averaging the different base models was already enough to improve the performance with regard to the base models. We also have seen that our approaches to create ensembles did not suffice to outperform the simple averaged ensemble. We have, however, successfully shown that combining the base models in a simple way improves performance; that the averaged model worked best just shows there is room for improvement, as we also have shown that type-dependent weights should perform better than type-independent weights.

Chapter 6

Conclusion and future work

Code-completion is a commonly used tool in today's IDEs. Prior work showed that the predictions of a code-completion assistant can be improved by analyzing and exploiting context information [Bru12][Ama13][HH11].

The goal of this thesis was to find context features from the Java byte code that are discriminative for method-call completion, and then combine them in an intelligent way to create models that are both small and an improvement of the state of the art.

In Section 2, we proposed several context features for improving code-completion assistants. Among those were the previously called methods, the method name of the surrounding method, the package name, and the parameter types of the surrounding method. To our knowledge, neither method name, nor package name, nor parameter types were previously examined in the context of method-call completion. In Section 3.4, we showed that the features we proposed are indeed discriminative and the base models based on those features outperform the frequency baseline. We also showed that all of the base models have types for which they work particularly well or bad, and none of them consistently outperforms the others for all types. We concluded that which part of the context helps the prediction most is type-dependent. We showed that method name and package name are surprisingly good features among the proposed ones. We attribute this to intra-project correlations.

In Section 5, we showed that using a weighted ensemble of the base models increases the average ranking performance. We found a simple averaging of the base models performed better than the other, more complicated approaches we suggested. We thus showed using more context information helps the prediction, even in a simple model. We did not conclusively show whether weighting should be type-dependent or type-independent, but still received some support for our thesis that weights should be type-dependent.

There are several things left open by this thesis that could be addressed by future work:

Since we found simple averaging to be superior to our other approaches, we showed that combining the base models by linear combination is a practicable approach. We just have not yet found the best way to find type-dependent weights. Future work could further investigate approaches to learn these weights. Possible candidates are state-of-the-art learning-to-rank methods like IntervalRank [MSCZ10] or Combined Ranking and Regression [Scu10].

The package-name model predicted surprisingly well. Future work should re-evaluate this model using a different test-training-data separation. We suggest that for properly testing this model, the test data should rather be separated along project boundaries. This would avoid that training and test data can come from the same package, which might be a contributor to the surprisingly good results of the package-name model. Also, the method-name model needs to be examined with regard to the influence of project naming conventions.

In our thesis, we only evaluated the models for the JRE types. To assert the validity of our observations, future work should evaluate the use of other libraries than the JRE. Libraries that have been used in prior work include, but are not limited to SWT [Bru12], Google Ads API [Ama13], Guava [Ama13], and Apache Maven [Ama13]. Also, different clients should be evaluated to assert the representativeness of our evaluation.

Although we stated expectations and assumptions about correlations between the different features, we did never directly investigate them. Future work could put further research effort in the correlation between the features. This may give further hints about what features are often redundant, and which features complement each other. For example, objects that come into scope as parameter of the method are used differently than objects that are created locally through a constructor invokation. We thus believe that there should be correlation of several features to the definition kind. Partitioning the data with regard to definition kind would be an easy way to evaluate how the definition kind plays together with other features, and weights dependend on the definition kind and not only on the type may prove to be superior to pure type-dependent weights.

Last but not least, code completion has additional context that we completely ignored: the prefix entered by the developer. Robbes et. al [RL08] included the prefix as a dimension of their evaluation. This was not an option for us as we already had the different types as additional dimension to be able to assert that different features are good for different types. The NDCG however is very abstract; evaluating again, this time with a less abstract metric and prefix-dependent, would give us a better idea about how good the presented models are on an absolute scale, rather than the relative scale of the NDCG.

Glossary

API	Application Programming Interface; consists of the classes and methods that are exposed to clients (as opposed to those that are only used internally)
base models	method-call recommendation model based on one feature or feature family
baseline	the most simple model that is compared to the other models; in the context of this thesis, the frequency model
code completion	autocomplete for source code
definition kind	feature describing the way by which an object entered the scope of the method; can be one of NEW, PARAMETER, METHOD_RETURN, FIELD, THIS and UNKNOWN
feature	observable variable
JRE	Java Runtime Environment (here: used as synonym for Java Runtime Library)
naive-Bayes assumption	assumption that implies a certain form of conditional independence between random variables
NDCG	normalized discounted cumulative gain; ranking metric
Simplex Algorithm	algorithm for solving linear optimization problems
statistical significance	describes that it is unlikely an experimental result was observed by chance

t-test   statistical hypothesis test; used to assert statistical significance

override context   the top-level definition of the surrounding method

List of Figures

References

[Ama13]   Sven Amann. Code Completion based on Implicit User Feedback, 2013.

[Bis06]   Christopher M. Bishop. *Pattern Recognition and Machine Learning*. Springer-Verlag, 2006.

[Blo]   Codetrails Blog. Codetrails connect 1.0.2 & new statistics on how you're using java apis. `http://www.codetrails.com/blog/codetrails-connect-102-new-statistics-how-youre-using-java-apis`. Webpage retrieved at 6 October 2013.

[Bru12]   Marcel Bruch. *IDE 2.0: Leveraging the Wisdom of the Software Engineering Crowds*. PhD thesis, 2012.

[BSS06]   Mokhtar S. Bazaraa, Hanif D. Sherali, and C. M. Shetty. *Nonlinear Programming: Theory And Algorithms*. Wiley-Interscience, May 2006.

[BT97]   Dimitris Bertsimas and John Tsitsiklis. *Introduction to Linear Optimization*. Athena Scientific, 1st edition, 1997.

[Com91]   Chemical Rubber Company. *CRC standard mathematical tables and formulae*. CRC Press, 1991.

[GVA06]   Nestor Garay-Vitoria and Julio Abascal. Text prediction systems: a survey. *Univers. Access Inf. Soc.*, 4(3):188--203, February 2006.

[HH11]   Lars Heinemann and Benjamin Hummel. Recommending api methods based on identifier contexts. In *Proceedings of the 3rd International Workshop on Search-Driven Development: Users, Infrastructure, Tools, and Evaluation*, SUITE '11, pages 1--4, New York, NY, USA, 2011. ACM.

[HWM09]   Sangmok Han, David R. Wallace, and Robert C. Miller. Code completion from abbreviated input. In *Proceedings of the 2009 IEEE/ACM International Conference on Automated Software Engineering*, ASE '09, pages 332--343, Washington, DC, USA, 2009. IEEE Computer Society.

[JK02]   Kalervo Järvelin and Jaana Kekäläinen. Cumulated gain-based evaluation of ir techniques. *ACM Trans. Inf. Syst.*, 20(4):422--446, October 2002.

[Lan04]   K. Lange. *Optimization*. Springer Texts in Statistics. Springer, 2004.

[MKF06]   Gail C. Murphy, Mik Kersten, and Leah Findlater. How are java software developers using the eclipse ide? *IEEE Software*, 23(4):76--83, 2006.

[MS99]   Christopher D. Manning and Hinrich Schütze. *Foundations of statistical natural language processing*. MIT Press, Cambridge, MA, USA, 1999.

[MSCZ10]   Taesup Moon, Alex Smola, Yi Chang, and Zhaohui Zheng. Intervalrank: isotonic regression with listwise and pairwise constraints. In *Proceedings of the third ACM international conference on Web search and data mining*, WSDM '10, pages 151--160, New York, NY, USA, 2010. ACM.

[Qui93]   J. Ross Quinlan. *C4.5: Programs for Machine Learning*. Morgan Kaufmann Publishers Inc., San Francisco, CA, USA, 1993.

[RL08]   R. Robbes and M. Lanza. How program history can improve code completion. In *Proceedings of the 2008 23rd IEEE/ACM International Conference on Automated Software Engineering*, ASE '08, pages 317--326, Washington, DC, USA, 2008. IEEE Computer Society.

[Scu10]   D. Sculley. Combined regression and ranking. In *Proceedings of the 16th ACM SIGKDD international conference on Knowledge discovery and data mining*, KDD '10, pages 979--988, New York, NY, USA, 2010. ACM.

[She07]   David J. Sheskin. *Handbook of Parametric and Nonparametric Statistical Procedures*. Chapman & Hall/CRC, 4 edition, 2007.

[Sho13]   Milad Shokouhi. Learning to personalize query auto-completion. In *Proceedings of the 36th international ACM SIGIR conference on Research and development in information retrieval*, SIGIR '13, pages 103--112, New York, NY, USA, 2013. ACM.

[SL]   Wouter Swierstra and Andres Löh. The semantics of version control. Submitted to POPL 2014.

[WKB09]   Markus Weimer, Alexandros Karatzoglou, and Marcel Bruch. Maximum margin matrix factorization for code recommendation. In *Proceedings of the third ACM conference on Recommender systems*, RecSys '09, pages 309--312, New York, NY, USA, 2009. ACM.

[Zha04]   Harry Zhang.   The Optimality of Naive Bayes.   In Valerie Barr and Zdravko Markov, editors, *FLAIRS Conference*. AAAI Press, 2004.